T0098290

A PRAYER FOR ALL

al-Jawshan
al-Kabir

A SUPPLICATION OF
PROPHET MUHAMMAD

www.tughrabooks.com

Translated by   Ali Ünal
Project Manager   Fikret Yaşar
Calligraphy (nash style) by   Betül Kırkan
Graphic design by   M. Sadık Kutlu
Gilding by   Ersan Perçem

Published by
Tughra Books
335 Clifton Ave, Clifton, NJ, 07011

ISBN: 978-1-59784-227-3

Al-Jawshan al-Kabir

The word *Jawshan* literally means breastplate, chain mail, or a similar type of armor. In Islamic terminology, it denotes a long prayer, known as *al-Jawshan al-Kabir*, transmitted from the Prophet.

Musa al-Kazim relates *al-Jawshan al-Kabir* from the Prophet on the successive authority of Ja'far al-Sadiq, Muhammad al-Bakir, Zayn al-Abidin, Husayn, and the fourth caliph, Ali.

Al-Jawshan al-Kabir is a long prayer consisting of one hundred parts. All parts, except a few, consist of ten of God's Names and Attributes. At the end of each part, this passage is repeated: *All-Glorified are You! There is no deity but You! Mercy! Mercy! Save (protect, deliver) us from the Fire!*

At the beginning of twenty-five of these one hundred parts, the phrase *I entreat You by Your Names* is found and these parts contain the Names of God that are invoked, such as "O God, O the All-Merciful, O the All-Compassionate." Within every part that begins with this phrase, there are various supplications beginning with expressions such as "O the Best of forgivers." Thus, the whole prayer comprises two-hundred-and-fifty Names of God and seven-hundred-and-fifty Attributes and supplications.

The main purpose of all these supplications is—as can be clearly understood from the content of the prayer and from the phrase *Mercy! Mercy! Protect us from the Fire!* repeated at the end of each part—to plead salvation from misfortune during this life and from punishment in the Hereafter.

Al-Jawshan al-Kabir is one of the prayers most frequently read by Muslims; various hadiths reported from the Prophet relate the rewards that one may receive in this world as well as in the Hereafter for reciting it. Some Muslims prefer to read the entire prayer by themselves, whereas others share it with their friends or household and make it a part of their daily service. Ahmed Ziyaeddin Gümüşhanevi included this prayer in his *Majmû'atü'l-Ahdhâb*, in which he collected many prayers that were repeatedly recited and formulas of remembrance of God. This prayer was published many times in separate volumes. In more recent times, it was made popular by Bediüzzaman Said Nursi (1877–1960), the author of the *Risale-i Nur* collection, a modern Qur'anic commentary.

Note: In Arabic, the direction of writing is from right to left; therefore pages start and flow in the same direction. This book also follows the same system, as the prayers were originally in Arabic. It should also be noted that number of each chapter comes after the prayer, not in the beginning; this is especially important when sharing chapters among several people.

الجوشن الكبير

الجوهر الثمين

الجوشن الكبير

بِسْمِ اللهِ الرَّحْمَنِ الرَّحِيمِ

اَللّهُمَّ اِنِّي اَسْاَلُكَ بِاَسْمَائِكَ يَا اللهُ ۞

يَا رَحْمنُ ۞ يَا رَحِيمُ ۞ يَا عَلِيمُ ۞ يَا حَلِيمُ ۞

يَا عَظِيمُ ۞ يَا حَكِيمُ ۞ يَا قَدِيمُ ۞ يَا مُقِيمُ ۞

يَا كَرِيمُ ۞

سُبْحَانَكَ يَا لَا اِلهَ اِلَّا اَنْتَ الْاَمَانَ الْاَمَانَ

خَلِّصْنَا مِنَ النَّارِ ۱

٤

1

1. O God, (the Divine Being Who creates and administers His creatures individually and as a whole; Who is Unique and Single, having no like or resemblance and to Whom nothing is comparable; Who is absolutely beyond any human conception and free from any imperfection; the Owner of the All-Beautiful Names, and the pure, sacred, eternal Attributes, and He Who has the exclusive right to worship,)

2. O the All-Merciful, (Who has mercy on the whole of existence and provides for them without making a distinction between believers and unbelievers,)

3. O the All-Compassionate, (Who has particular compassion for each of His creatures in their maintenance, and for His believing servants, especially in the other world,)

4. O the All-Knowing, (Whose Knowledge encompasses everything down to the smallest and from Whom nothing is hidden,)

5. O the All-Clement and Forbearing, (Who shows no haste to punish the errors of His servants,)

6. O the All-Supreme and Tremendous,

7. O the All-Wise, (in Whose every act and decree there are many instances of wisdom,)

8. O the Pre-Eternally Existent, (Who exists without having a beginning,)

9. O the All-Enduring, (Who has existed and will exist eternally with no cessation and Who maintains all that exists,)

10. O the All-Munificent, (Whose goodness is abundant, Whose gifts are endless and Who possesses all honor and virtue,)

All-Glorified are You; there is no deity but You!
Mercy! Mercy! Save us from the Fire!

يَا مُجِيبَ الدَّعَوَاتِ ۞ يَا سَيِّدَ السَّادَاتِ ۞

يَا رَفِيعَ الدَّرَجَاتِ ۞ يَا وَلِيَّ الْحَسَنَاتِ ۞

يَا غَافِرَ الْخَطِيئَاتِ ۞ يَا عَظِيمَ الْبَرَكَاتِ ۞

يَا سَامِعَ الْأَصْوَاتِ ۞ يَا دَافِعَ الْبَلِيَّاتِ ۞

يَا مُعْطِيَ الْمَسْئُولَاتِ ۞

يَا عَالِمَ السِّرِّ وَالْخَفِيَّاتِ ۞

سُبْحَانَكَ يَا لَا إِلَهَ إِلَّا أَنْتَ الْأَمَانَ الْأَمَانَ

خَلِّصْنَا مِنَ النَّارِ ۞

يَا خَيْرَ النَّاصِرِينَ ۞ يَا خَيْرَ الْغَافِرِينَ ۞

يَا خَيْرَ الْفَاتِحِينَ ۞ يَا خَيْرَ الْحَاكِمِينَ ۞

يَا خَيْرَ الْوَارِثِينَ ۞ يَا خَيْرَ الذَّاكِرِينَ ۞

٥

2

1. O Master of masters,
2. O He Who answers all prayers,
3. O He Who is the dealer, preserver and bestower of all good,
4. O He Who is above all conceivable ranks and Who elevates the ranks of His believing, devoted servants,
5. O He Who is supreme and tremendous in blessings,
6. O He Who forgives mistakes and faults,
7. O He Who repels all calamities,
8. O He Who hears all the voices (from all beings, be they weak or strong, hidden or articulated, without confusion,)
9. O He Who grants the needs and desires of all creatures,
10. O He Who knows all secrets and all hidden things,

All-Glorified are You; there is no deity but You!
Mercy! Mercy! Save us from the Fire!

3

1. O He Who is uniquely best in forgiving,
2. O He Who is uniquely best in helping,
3. O He Who is uniquely best in ruling and judging,
4. O He Who is uniquely best in opening the ways or doors of good, success, and prosperity,
5. O He Who is uniquely best in mentioning, Who mentions His believing, obedient servants in high assemblies,
6. O He Who is uniquely best in inheriting the deceased and their deeds and preserving legacies.

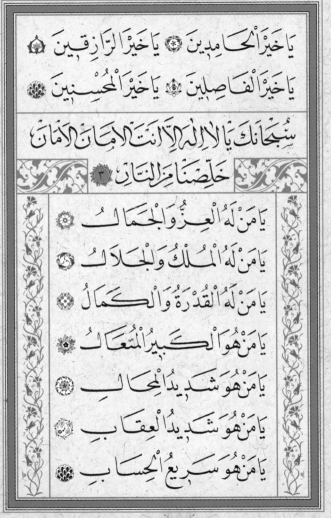

يَا خَيْرَ الْحَامِدِينَ ❀ يَا خَيْرَ الرَّازِقِينَ ❀

يَا خَيْرَ الْفَاصِلِينَ ❀ يَا خَيْرَ الْمُحْسِنِينَ

سُبْحَانَكَ يَا لَا إِلَهَ إِلَّا أَنْتَ الْأَمَانَ الْأَمَانَ

خَلِّصْنَا مِنَ النَّارِ ۳

يَا مَنْ لَهُ الْعِزُّ وَالْجَمَالُ ❀

يَا مَنْ لَهُ الْمُلْكُ وَالْجَلَالُ ❀

يَا مَنْ لَهُ الْقُدْرَةُ وَالْكَمَالُ ❀

يَا مَنْ هُوَ الْكَبِيرُ الْمُتَعَالُ ❀

يَا مَنْ هُوَ شَدِيدُ الْمِحَالِ ❀

يَا مَنْ هُوَ شَدِيدُ الْعِقَابِ ❀

يَا مَنْ هُوَ سَرِيعُ الْحِسَابِ ❀

7. O He Who is uniquely best in praising and giving the reward to those who praise Him,

8. O He Who is uniquely best in providing for beings,

9. O He Who is uniquely best in discerning the truth from falsehood and judging between them,

10. O He Who is the uniquely best in benevolence and doing good,

All-Glorified are You; there is no deity but You!
Mercy! Mercy! Save us from the Fire!

4

1. O He to Whom belong absolute might and glory and absolute grace and beauty

2. O He to Whom belong absolute sovereignty and majesty,

3. O He to Whom belong absolute Power and Perfection,

4. O He Who is the All-Great, the All-Transcending,

5. O He Who is most severe in penalizing,

6. O He Who is most severe in punishing,

7. O He Who is most swift in reckoning,

يَا مَنْ هُوَ عِنْدَهُ حُسْنُ الثَّوَابِ ۞

يَا مَنْ هُوَ عِنْدَهُ أُمُّ الْكِتَابِ ۞

يَا مَنْ هُوَ يُنْشِئُ السَّحَابَ الثِّقَالَ ۞

سُبْحَانَكَ يَا لَا إِلَهَ إِلَّا أَنْتَ الْأَمَانَ الْأَمَانَ

خَلِّصْنَا مِنَ النَّارِ ۞ ٤

وَأَسْأَلُكَ بِأَسْمَائِكَ يَا حَنَّانُ ۞ يَا مَنَّانُ ۞

يَا دَيَّانُ ۞ يَا غُفْرَانُ ۞ يَا بُرْهَانُ ۞

يَا سُلْطَانُ ۞ يَا سُبْحَانُ ۞ يَا مُسْتَعَانُ ۞

يَا ذَا الْمَنِّ وَالْبَيَانِ ۞ يَا ذَا الْأَمَانِ ۞

سُبْحَانَكَ يَا لَا إِلَهَ إِلَّا أَنْتَ الْأَمَانَ الْأَمَانَ

خَلِّصْنَا مِنَ النَّارِ ۞ ٥

٧

8. O He with Whom is the best of rewards,
9. O He with Whom is the Mother of all books,
10. O He Who creates clouds of rain,

All-Glorified are You; there is no deity but You!
Mercy! Mercy! Save us from the Fire!

5

I entreat You by Your Names:

1. O the All-Kind and Caring, (Who manifests Himself with His Mercy and is inclined [even] toward those who turn away from Him,)
2. O the All-Bounteous and Favoring,
3. O the Supreme Ruler and All-Requiting (of good and evil),
4. O the All-Forgiving of sins,
5. O the All-Proving and Demonstrating,
6. O the Absolute, Eternal Authority,
7. O the All-Glorified, Who is absolutely free from all deficiencies and imperfections and from doing anything wrong or in vain,
8. O He Whose help is always sought,
9. O the Owner of all bounty and goodness and eternal exposition, (Who nourishes His creatures with His infinite blessings, and Who communicates His decrees to all His creatures in the most perfectly eloquent way,)
10. O He Whose protection is sufficient against all fear and danger,

All-Glorified are You; there is no deity but You!
Mercy! Mercy! Save us from the Fire!

يَا مَنْ تَوَاضَعَ كُلُّ شَيْءٍ لِعَظَمَتِهِ ۞

يَا مَنِ اسْتَسْلَمَ كُلُّ شَيْءٍ لِقُدْرَتِهِ ۞

يَا مَنْ ذَلَّ كُلُّ شَيْءٍ لِعِزَّتِهِ ۞

يَا مَنْ خَضَعَ كُلُّ شَيْءٍ لِهَيْبَتِهِ ۞

يَا مَنِ انْقَادَ كُلُّ شَيْءٍ لِمُلْكِهِ ۞

يَا مَنْ دَانَ كُلُّ شَيْءٍ مِنْ مَخَافَتِهِ ۞

يَا مَنِ انْشَقَّتِ الْجِبَالُ مِنْ خَشْيَتِهِ ۞

يَا مَنْ قَامَتِ السَّمَوَاتُ بِأَمْرِهِ ۞

يَا مَنِ اسْتَقَرَّتِ الْأَرْضُ بِإِذْنِهِ ۞

يَا مَنْ لَا يَعْتَدِي عَلَى أَهْلِ مَمْلَكَتِهِ ۞

سُبْحَانَكَ يَا لَا إِلَهَ إِلَّا أَنْتَ الْأَمَانُ الْأَمَانُ

6

1. O He before Whose Grandeur all things yield,
2. O He before Whose Power all things submit,
3. O He before Whose Glory and Might all things bow and obey,
4. O He before Whose Magnificence all things stand in reverent humility,
5. O He to Whose Sovereignty all things are subservient,
6. O He in fearful awe of Whom all things bow in obedience,
7. O He in reverent awe of Whom mountains crumble,
8. O He by Whose command the firmaments were raised and fixed,
9. O He by Whose permission the earth found stability,
10. O He Who never violates the rights of the people of His Kingdom,

All-Glorified are You; there is no deity but You!
Mercy! Mercy! Save us from the Fire!

خَلِّصْنَا مِنَ النَّارِ ٦

يَا غَافِرَ الْخَطَايَا ۞ يَا كَاشِفَ الْبَلَايَا ۞

يَا مُنْتَهَى الرَّجَايَا ۞ يَا مُجْزِلَ الْعَطَايَا ۞

يَا وَاسِعَ الْهَدَايَا ۞ يَا رَازِقَ الْبَرَايَا ۞

يَا قَاضِيَ الْمَنَايَا ۞ يَا سَامِعَ الشَّكَايَا ۞

يَا بَاعِثَ السَّرَايَا ۞ يَا مُطْلِقَ الْأُسَارَى ۞

سُبْحَانَكَ يَا لَا إِلٰهَ إِلَّا أَنْتَ الْأَمَانَ الْأَمَانَ

خَلِّصْنَا مِنَ النَّارِ ٧

يَا ذَا الْحَمْدِ وَالثَّنَاءِ ۞ يَا ذَا الْمَجْدِ وَالسَّنَاءِ ۞

يَا ذَا الْفَخْرِ وَالْبَهَاءِ ۞ يَا ذَا الْعَهْدِ وَالْوَفَاءِ ۞

يَا ذَا الْعَفْوِ وَالرِّضَاءِ ۞ يَا ذَا الْمَنِّ وَالْعَطَاءِ ۞

٩

7

1. O the Forgiver of errors,
2. O the Remover of calamities,
3. O the Final Resort for needs and desires,
4. O He Whose favors are plenteous,
5. O He whose gifts are bounteous,
6. O He Who provides for all creatures,
7. O He Who determines the time to die and carries it out on time,
8. O He Who hears complaints,
9. O He who sends armies to save the needy,
10. O He Who frees those who are in physical and spiritual captivity,

All-Glorified are You; there is no deity but You!
Mercy! Mercy! Save us from the Fire!

8

1. O He Who is eternally and deservedly thanked and praised,
2. O He Who is the owner of all glory, honor, and sublimity,
3. O He Who deserves infinite praise and Who is the owner of all that is sublime and valuable,
4. O He Who always keeps His promises and Who fulfills them in the best manner,
5. O He Who forgives and Who is pleased with those who seek His forgiveness and good pleasure,
6. O He Whose bounty and gifts to His creatures are without measure,

يَا ذَا الْفَصْلِ وَالْقَضَاءِ ۞ يَا ذَا الْعِزَّةِ وَالْبَقَاءِ ۞

يَا ذَا الْجُوْدِ وَالنَّعْمَاءِ ۞ يَا ذَا الْفَضْلِ وَالْآلاءِ ۞

سُبْحَانَكَ يَا لَا إِلٰهَ إِلَّا أَنْتَ الْأَمَانَ الْأَمَانَ

خَلِّصْنَا مِنَ النَّارِ ۞ ٨

وَأَسْأَلُكَ بِأَسْمَائِكَ يَا مَانِعُ ۞ يَا دَافِعُ ۞

يَا نَافِعُ ۞ يَا سَامِعُ ۞ يَا رَافِعُ ۞ يَا صَانِعُ ۞

يَا شَافِعُ ۞ يَا جَامِعُ ۞ يَا وَاسِعُ ۞ يَا مُوَسِّعُ ۞

سُبْحَانَكَ يَا لَا إِلٰهَ إِلَّا أَنْتَ الْأَمَانَ الْأَمَانَ

خَلِّصْنَا مِنَ النَّارِ ۞ ٩

يَا صَانِعَ كُلِّ مَصْنُوعٍ ۞

يَا خَالِقَ كُلِّ مَخْلُوقٍ

7. O He to Whom belong the solution of every matter and the execution of every rule and judgment,
8. O He Who is everlasting with infinite honor and might,
9. O He Who grants His blessings with generosity,
10. O He Who gives abundantly without expecting anything in return,

All-Glorified are You; there is no deity but You!
Mercy! Mercy! Save us from the Fire!

9

I entreat You by Your Names:
1. O the All-Withholding, Who prevents anything He does not will,
2. O the All-Repelling, Who removes and keeps away anything from whatever He wills,
3. O the Creator of things beneficial, Who gives to whomever He wills as He wills,
4. O the All-Hearing,
5. O the All-Exalting, Who Himself is exalted in every way, and Who exalts whomever He wills,
6. O the Maker, Who makes all things with perfect art,
7. O the All-Interceding, Who intercedes on behalf of whomever He wills, and accepts the intercession of whomever He wills,
8. O the All-Gathering Who collects all goodness and beauty in Himself, and Who will gather all responsible beings in His Presence at the time of the Resurrection,
9. O the All-Embracing, Who embraces everything in knowledge, power, and mercy,
10. O the All-Expanding, Who expands to whatever extent He wills,

All-Glorified are You; there is no deity but You!
Mercy! Mercy! Save us from the Fire!

10

1. O the Maker of all that is made with perfect art,
2. O the Creator of all that is created,

يَا رَازِقَ كُلِّ مَرْزُوقٍ ۞

يَا مَالِكَ كُلِّ مَمْلُوكٍ ۞

يَا كَاشِفَ كُلِّ مَكْرُوبٍ ۞

يَا فَارِجَ كُلِّ مَغْمُومٍ ۞

يَا رَاحِمَ كُلِّ مَرْحُومٍ ۞

يَا نَاصِرَ كُلِّ مَخْذُولٍ ۞

يَا سَاتِرَ كُلِّ مَعْيُوبٍ ۞

يَا مَلْجَأَ كُلِّ مَظْلُومٍ ۞

سُبْحَانَكَ يَا لَا إِلٰهَ إِلَّا أَنْتَ الْأَمَانَ الْأَمَانَ
خَلِّصْنَا مِنَ النَّارِ ۞ ۱۰

يَا عُدَّتِي عِنْدَ شِدَّتِي ۞

3. O He Who provides for all things that are in need of sustenance,

4. O the Master of all that is owned (by Him),

5. O He Who comforts all who are in trouble,

6. O He Who relieves all who are in gloom and despair,

7. O He Who has compassion on those who are in need of compassion,

8. O He Who helps all those who are devoid of help,

9. O He Who veils all shame,

10. O the Constant-Refuge of all who are oppressed,

All-Glorified are You; there is no deity but You!
Mercy! Mercy! Save us from the Fire!

11

1. O He Who is my helper and support when I fall upon hard times,

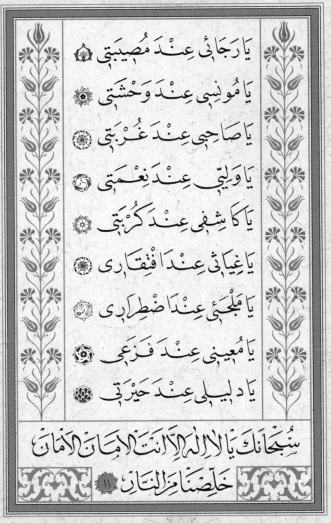

يَا رَجَائِى عِنْدَ مُصِيبَتِى ۞

يَا مُونِسِى عِنْدَ وَحْشَتِى ۞

يَا صَاحِبِى عِنْدَ غُرْبَتِى ۞

يَا وَلِيِّى عِنْدَ نِعْمَتِى ۞

يَا كَاشِفِى عِنْدَ كُرْبَتِى ۞

يَا غِيَاثِى عِنْدَ افْتِقَارِى ۞

يَا مَلْجَئِى عِنْدَ اضْطِرَارِى ۞

يَا مُعِينِى عِنْدَ فَزَعِى ۞

يَا دَلِيلِى عِنْدَ حَيْرَتِى ۞

سُبْحَانَكَ يَا لَا اِلٰهَ اِلَّا اَنْتَ الْاَمَانَ الْاَمَانَ

خَلِّصْنَا مِنَ النَّارِ ۞ ١١

2. O He Who is my source of hope when misfortune falls upon me,

3. O He Who is my companion when I am lonely and desolate,

4. O He Who supports me with His mercy, protection, and patronage when I am far from home and lonely,

5. O my Guardian, Who is the only source of all the blessings that I enjoy,

6. O the Remover of my grief and troubles,

7. O my Succor Who helps me when I am in need,

8. O my Refuge when troubles and hard times befall me,

9. O my Helper when I am afraid,

10. O my Guide to the right path when I am baffled and confused,

All-Glorified are You; there is no deity but You!
Mercy! Mercy! Save us from the Fire!

يَا غَفَّارَ الذُّنُوبِ ❋ يَا عَلَّامَ الْغُيُوبِ ❋

يَا كَشَّافَ الْكُرُوبِ ❋ يَا سَتَّارَ الْعُيُوبِ ❋

يَا مُزَيِّنَ الْقُلُوبِ ❋ يَا مُقَلِّبَ الْقُلُوبِ ❋

يَا طَبِيبَ الْقُلُوبِ ❋ يَا مُنَوِّرَ الْقُلُوبِ ❋

يَا أَنِيسَ الْقُلُوبِ ❋ يَا حَبِيبَ الْقُلُوبِ ❋

سُبْحَانَكَ يَا لَا إِلَهَ إِلَّا أَنْتَ الْأَمَانَ الْأَمَانَ

خَلِّصْنَا مِنَ النَّارِ ﴿١٢﴾

وَأَسْأَلُكَ بِأَسْمَائِكَ يَا جَلِيلُ ❋ يَا جَمِيلُ ❋

يَا وَكِيلُ ❋ يَا كَفِيلُ ❋ يَا دَلِيلُ ❋ يَا مُقِيلُ ❋

يَا خَبِيرُ ❋ يَا لَطِيفُ ❋ يَا عَزِيزُ ❋ يَا مَلِيكُ ❋

سُبْحَانَكَ يَا لَا إِلَهَ إِلَّا أَنْتَ الْأَمَانَ الْأَمَانَ

١٣

1. O the All-Knowing of all that is Unseen,
2. O the All-Forgiving of sins,
3. O the All-Veiling of shame,
4. O the All-Removing of grief and trouble,
5. O He Who changes hearts from one state to another,
6. O He Who adorns hearts (with piety, righteousness, and virtue),
7. O He Who illuminates hearts (with the light of belief and Qur'an),
8. O the Hearer of hearts,
9. O the Beloved of hearts,
10. O the Intimate Companion of hearts,

All-Glorified are You; there is no deity but You!
Mercy! Mercy! Save us from the Fire!

I entreat You by Your Names:
1. O the All-Majestic, (Who is the One of infinite grandeur),
2. O the All-Beautiful and Gracious,
3. O the One to rely on and the One to Whom affairs should be entrusted,
4. O the Guarantor, (Who assumes the provision of the needs of creatures,)
5. O the All-Evidence for the truth, (Who shows the true path to His servants,)
6. O the All-Pardoning, (Who forgives the faults of His servants,)
7. O the All-Aware, (from Whom nothing remains hidden,)
8. O the All-Gracious and Subtle, (Who provides abundantly and graciously, and penetrates into the most minute dimensions of all things),
9. O the All-Glorious with irresistible might (Whom none can prevent from doing what He wills),
10. O the absolute Sovereign,

All-Glorified are You; there is no deity but You!
Mercy! Mercy! Save us from the Fire!

يَا دَلِيلَ الْمُتَحَيِّرِينَ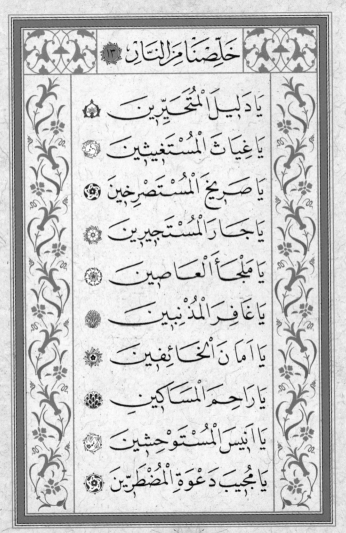

يَا غِيَاثَ الْمُسْتَغِيثِينَ

يَا صَرِيخَ الْمُسْتَصْرِخِينَ

يَا جَارَ الْمُسْتَجِيرِينَ

يَا مَلْجَأَ الْعَاصِينَ

يَا غَافِرَ الْمُذْنِبِينَ

يَا آمَانَ الْخَائِفِينَ

يَا رَاحِمَ الْمَسَاكِينِ

يَا أَنِيسَ الْمُسْتَوْحِشِينَ

يَا مُجِيبَ دَعْوَةِ الْمُضْطَرِّينَ

1. O He Who is All-Evidence and the Guide for the bewildered,

2. O the Helper of those who ask for help,

3. O the Savior of those who ask for deliverance,

4. O the Protector of those who seek protection,

5. O the Refuge of the rebellious,

6. O the Forgiver of sinners,

7. O He with Whom the fearful seek refuge and Who gives them security,

8. O He Who is compassionate to the helpless and needy,

9. O the intimate Companion of those who are desolate and those who have no one to whom they can turn,

10. O He Who answers the prayers of those in desperate straits,

سُبْحَانَكَ يَا لَا اِلٰهَ اِلَّا اَنْتَ الْاَمَانَ الْاَمَانَ
خَلِّصْنَا مِنَ النَّارِ ۝١٤

يَا ذَا الْجُوْدِ وَالْاِحْسَانِ ۝

يَا ذَا الْفَضْلِ وَالْاِمْتِنَانِ ۝

يَا ذَا الْاَمْنِ وَالْاَمَانِ ۝

يَا ذَا الْقُدْسِ وَالسُّبْحَانِ ۝

يَا ذَا الْحِكْمَةِ وَالْبَيَانِ ۝

يَا ذَا الرَّحْمَةِ وَالرِّضْوَانِ ۝

يَا ذَا الْحُجَّةِ وَالْبُرْهَانِ ۝

يَا ذَا الْعَظَمَةِ وَالسُّلْطَانِ ۝

يَا ذَا الْعَفْوِ وَالْغُفْرَانِ ۝

All-Glorified are You; there is no deity but You!
Mercy! Mercy! Save us from the Fire!

15

1. O the One of infinite generosity and favors,

2. O He Who gives blessings out of His grace without expecting anything in return,

3. O He Who provides safety and security,

4. O the One of absolute purity and holiness, and absolute freedom from any fault or imperfection, and from having partners, equals, or opposites,

5. O the One of absolute wisdom and perfect articulation,

6. O He Who is infinitely merciful to His creatures and is pleased with His obedient servants,

7. O He Who brings about the existence of all things and Who is the proof and evidence of His existence as well as His creation,

8. O the One of limitless grandeur and absolute authority,

9. O He Who pardons, grants remission and excuses, and Who forgives,

يَا ذَا الرَّأْفَةِ وَالْمُسْتَعَانِ ۞

سُبْحَانَكَ يَا لَا إِلَهَ إِلَّا أَنْتَ الْأَمَانَ الْأَمَانَ

خَلِّصْنَا مِنَ النَّارِ ۞ ١٥

يَا مَنْ هُوَ رَبُّ كُلِّ شَيْءٍ ۞

يَا مَنْ هُوَ إِلَهُ كُلِّ شَيْءٍ ۞

يَا مَنْ هُوَ خَالِقُ كُلِّ شَيْءٍ ۞

يَا مَنْ هُوَ فَوْقَ كُلِّ شَيْءٍ ۞

يَا مَنْ هُوَ قَبْلَ كُلِّ شَيْءٍ ۞

يَا مَنْ هُوَ بَعْدَ كُلِّ شَيْءٍ ۞

يَا مَنْ هُوَ عَالِمٌ كُلِّ شَيْءٍ ۞

يَا مَنْ هُوَ قَادِرٌ كُلِّ شَيْءٍ ۞

10. O the One of infinite affection to Whom every living being turns for help,

All-Glorified are You; there is no deity but You!
Mercy! Mercy! Save us from the Fire!

16

1. O He Who is the Lord of all things,
2. O He Who is the Deity of all things,
3. O He Who is the Creator of all things,
4. O He Who is transcendently above all things,
5. O He Who pre-eternally existed before all things,
6. O He Who will eternally survive all things,
7. O He Who is the All-Knowing of all things,
8. O He Who is the All-Powerful over all things,

يَا مَنْ هُوَ صَانِعُ كُلِّ شَيْءٍ ۞

يَا مَنْ هُوَ يَبْقَى وَيُفْنَى كُلُّ شَيْءٍ ۞

سُبْحَانَكَ يَا لَا إِلَهَ إِلَّا أَنْتَ الْأَمَانَ الْأَمَانَ

خَلِّصْنَا مِنَ النَّارِ ﴿١٦﴾

وَأَسْأَلُكَ بِأَسْمَائِكَ يَا مُؤْمِنُ ۞ يَا مُهَيْمِنُ

يَا مُكَوِّنُ ۞ يَا مُلَقِّنُ ۞ يَا مُبِينُ ۞ يَا مُهَوِّنُ

يَا مُزَيِّنُ ۞ يَا مُعَظِّمُ ۞ يَا مُعِينُ ۞ يَا مُلَوِّنُ ۞

سُبْحَانَكَ يَا لَا إِلَهَ إِلَّا أَنْتَ الْأَمَانَ الْأَمَانَ

خَلِّصْنَا مِنَ النَّارِ ﴿١٧﴾

يَا مَنْ هُوَ فِي مُلْكِهِ مُقِيمٌ ۞

يَا مَنْ هُوَ فِي جَلَالِهِ عَظِيمٌ

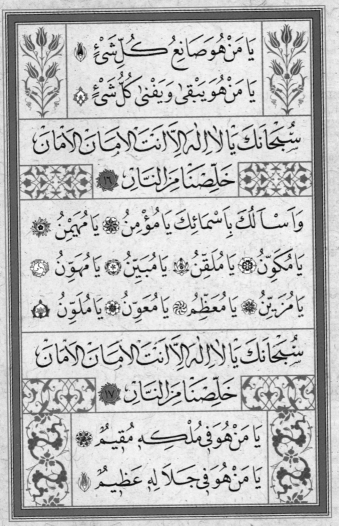

9. O He Who makes all things with perfect art,
10. O He Who exists permanently, while all else is subject to perishing,

All-Glorified are You; there is no deity but You!
Mercy! Mercy! Save us from the Fire!

17

I entreat You by Your Names:

1. O the Supreme Author of safety and security Who bestows faith and removes all doubt,
2. O the All-Watchful Guardian, (Who protects His servants and watches over what they do,)
3. O He Who brings everything into existence with the single command of "Be!",
4. O the All-Instructing Who inspires and teaches His creatures what they need,
5. O He Who explains everything that needs explanation and communicates His decrees in clear terms,
6. O the All-Facilitating (Who makes all manner of difficult things easy for His servants,)
7. O the All-Adorning (Who adorns all things in the most suitable fashion,)
8. O the All-Supreme (Whose grandeur is acknowledged by His servants,)
9. O the All-Aiding (Who makes His creatures assist one another and Who helps those who are in need,)
10. O the All-Coloring, (Who beautifies all things by creating them in various kinds and colors,)

All-Glorified are You; there is no deity but You!
Mercy! Mercy! Save us from the Fire!

18

1. O He Who is enduring in His Kingdom,
2. O He Who is supreme in His Majesty,

يَا مَنْ هُوَ فِي سُلْطَانِهِ قَدِيمٌ ۞

يَا مَنْ هُوَ عَلَى عَبْدِهِ رَحِيمٌ ۞

يَا مَنْ هُوَ بِكُلِّ شَئٍ عَلِيمٌ ۞

يَا مَنْ هُوَ لِمَنْ جَفَاهُ حَلِيمٌ ۞

يَا مَنْ هُوَ لِمَنْ تَرَجَّاهُ كَرِيمٌ ۞

يَا مَنْ هُوَ فِي مَقَادِيرِهِ حَكِيمٌ ۞

يَا مَنْ هُوَ فِي حُكْمِهِ لَطِيفٌ ۞

يَا مَنْ هُوَ فِي لُطْفِهِ قَدِيرٌ ۞

سُبْحَانَكَ يَا لَا إِلَهَ إِلَّا أَنْتَ الْأَمَانَ الْأَمَانَ

خَلِّصْنَا مِنَ النَّارِ ۱۸

يَا مَنْ لَا يُرْجَى إِلَّا فَضْلُهُ ۞

3. O He Who is pre-eternal in His authority,

4. O He Who is compassionate for His servants,

5. O He Who has perfect knowledge of all things,

6. O He Who is clement toward those who turn away from Him in offense,

7. O He Who is magnanimous toward those who put their trust in Him,

8. O He Who is wise in His providence, measures, judgments, and ordinances,

9. O He Who is gracious and subtle in His rule,

10. O He Who is powerful in His graciousness and subtlety,

All-Glorified are You; there is no deity but You!
Mercy! Mercy! Save us from the Fire!

19

1. O He Whose grace and favors are expected,

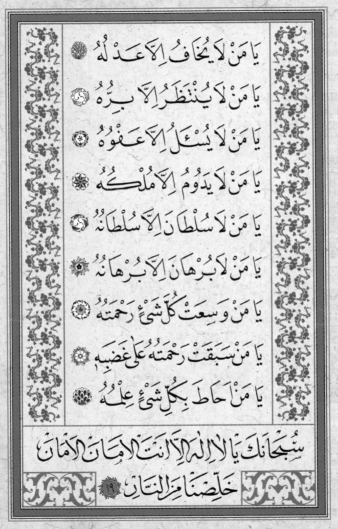

يَا مَنْ لَا يَخَافُ اِلَّا الْعَدْلَهُ ۞

يَا مَنْ لَا يَنْتَظِرُ اِلَّا بِرَّهُ ۞

يَا مَنْ لَا يَسْئَلُ اِلَّا عَفْوَهُ ۞

يَا مَنْ لَا يَدُومُ اِلَّا مُلْكَهُ ۞

يَا مَنْ لَا سُلْطَانَ اِلَّا سُلْطَانُهُ ۞

يَا مَنْ لَا بُرْهَانَ اِلَّا بُرْهَانُهُ ۞

يَا مَنْ وَسِعَتْ كُلَّ شَيْءٍ رَحْمَتُهُ ۞

يَا مَنْ سَبَقَتْ رَحْمَتُهُ عَلَى غَضَبِهِ ۞

يَا مَنْ اَحَاطَ بِكُلِّ شَيْءٍ عِلْمُهُ ۞

سُبْحَانَكَ يَا لَا اِلٰهَ اِلَّا اَنْتَ الْاَمَانَ الْاَمَانَ

خَلِّصْنَا مِنَ النَّارِ ۱۹ ۞

2. O He Whose justice is feared, (as we deserve punishment and it is only His pure grace and forgiveness which will save us from this,)

3. O He Whose goodness and beneficence are anticipated,

4. O He Whose overlooking of faults and pardoning is desired,

5. O He Who has the only Kingdom that will endure permanently,

6. O He Whose Authority is the only true authority,

7. O He Whose Evidence is the only evidence which is exclusively sufficient for the truth of everything that is true,

8. O He Whose Mercy embraces everything,

9. O He Whose Mercy surpasses His Wrath,

10. O He Whose Knowledge encompasses everything,

All-Glorified are You; there is no deity but You!
Mercy! Mercy! Save us from the Fire!

يَا كَاشِفَ الْغَمِّ ۞ يَا فَارِجَ الْهَمِّ ۞

يَا قَابِلَ التَّوْبِ ۞ يَا غَافِرَ الذَّنْبِ ۞

يَا صَادِقَ الْوَعْدِ ۞ يَا خَالِقَ الْخَلْقِ ۞

يَا مُوفِيَ الْعَهْدِ ۞ يَا رَازِقَ الطِّفْلِ ۞

يَا فَالِقَ الْحَبِّ ۞ يَا عَالِمَ السِّرِّ ۞

سُبْحَانَكَ يَا لَا إِلَهَ إِلَّا أَنْتَ الْأَمَانُ الْأَمَانُ

خَلِّصْنَا مِنَ النَّارِ ۞

فَأَسْأَلُكَ بِأَسْمَائِكَ يَا عَلِيُّ ۞ يَا وَفِيُّ ۞

يَا زَكِيُّ ۞ يَا مَلِيُّ ۞ يَا غَنِيُّ ۞ يَا وَلِيُّ ۞

يَا قَوِيُّ ۞ يَا حَفِيُّ ۞ يَا بَدِيُّ ۞ يَا رَضِيُّ ۞

سُبْحَانَكَ يَا لَا إِلَهَ إِلَّا أَنْتَ الْأَمَانُ الْأَمَانُ

1. O the Eliminator of troubles and worries,
2. O the Remover of sorrow and anxieties,
3. O the Forgiver of sins,
4. O the Acceptor of repentance,
5. O the Creator of all creation,
6. O He Who is truthful in His promise,
7. O He Who provides for infants affectionately,
8. O He Who fulfills His covenants,
9. O the Knower of all secrets,
10. O the Splitter of seeds and kernels to make them sprout,

All-Glorified are You; there is no deity but You!
Mercy! Mercy! Save us from the Fire!

21

I entreat You by Your Names:

1. O the All-Exalted,
2. O the All-Faithful (Who is truthful in His promises),
3. O the All-Guardian, the All-Protecting Friend (to rely on),
4. O the All-Wealthy and Self-Sufficient,
5. O the Owner of infinite treasures,
6. O the All-Pure, (Who is free from any imperfection or impurity),
7. O the All-Pleased, (Who makes Himself loved by His servants through His blessings and is pleased with their obedience),
8. O the All-Manifest, (Who is more manifest than anything else),
9. O the All-Hidden, (Who is hidden due to the dazzling density of His manifestation, and Who knows everything down to the finest details and has hidden favors,)
10. O the All-Strong,

يَا مَنْ أَظْهَرَ الْجَمِيلَ ۞

يَا مَنْ سَتَرَ الْقَبِيحَ ۞

يَا مَنْ لَا يُؤَاخِذُ بِالْجَرِيمَةِ ۞

يَا مَنْ لَا يَهْتِكُ السِّتْرَ ۞

يَا عَظِيمَ الْعَفْوِ ۞

يَا حَسَنَ التَّجَاوُزِ ۞

يَا وَاسِعَ الْمَغْفِرَةِ ۞

يَا بَاسِطَ الْيَدَيْنِ بِالرَّحْمَةِ ۞

يَا صَاحِبَ كُلِّ نَجْوَى ۞

يَا مُنْتَهَى كُلِّ شَكْوَى ۞

All-Glorified are You; there is no deity but You!
Mercy! Mercy! Save us from the Fire!

22

1. O He Who manifests the beautiful,

2. O He Who covers the ugly,

3. O He Who is not harmed by the crimes of His servants and Who makes not haste to punish them in revenge,

4. O He Who does not tear apart the veil of secret shame,

5. O the One of supreme pardoning and dispensation,

6. O He Who overlooks the faults of His servants mercifully and beautifully,

7. O the One of all-extensive forgiveness,

8. O He Whose both "hands" are open with mercy,

9. O He Who hears and knows every whisper and secret counsel,

10. O He Who is the ultimate authority for all complaints,

سُبْحَانَكَ يَا لَا إِلٰهَ إِلَّا أَنْتَ الْأَمَانَ الْأَمَانَ

خَلِّصْنَا مِنَ النَّارِ ۞

يَا ذَا النِّعْمَةِ السَّابِغَةِ ۞

يَا ذَا الرَّحْمَةِ الْوَاسِعَةِ ۞

يَا ذَا الْحِكْمَةِ الْبَالِغَةِ ۞

يَا ذَا الْقُدْرَةِ الْكَامِلَةِ ۞

يَا ذَا الْحُجَّةِ الْقَاطِعَةِ ۞

يَا ذَا الْكَرَامَةِ الظَّاهِرَةِ ۞

يَا ذَا الصِّفَةِ الْعَالِيَةِ ۞

يَا ذَا الْعِزَّةِ الدَّائِمَةِ ۞

يَا ذَا الْقُوَّةِ الْمَتِينَةِ ۞

All-Glorified are You; there is no deity but You!
Mercy! Mercy! Save us from the Fire!

23

1. O the One of all-embracing bounty and blessings,
2. O the One of all-extensive mercy,
3. O the One of complete, all-encompassing wisdom,
4. O the One of perfect power,
5. O the One of decisive proof,
6. O the One of manifest generosity and goodness,
7. O the One of all-sublime attributes,
8. O the One of never-ending glory and might,
9. O the One of firm and unshakable strength,

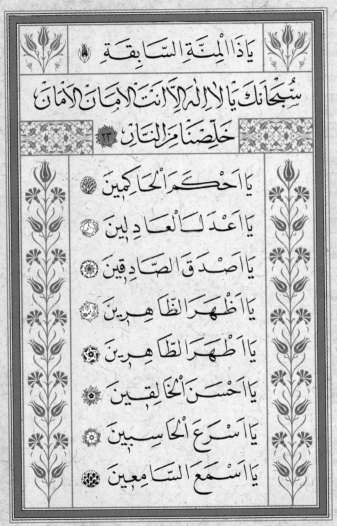

يَا ذَا الْمِنَّةِ السَّابِقَةِ ۩

سُبْحَانَكَ يَا لَا إِلٰهَ إِلَّا أَنْتَ الْأَمَانَ الْأَمَانَ
خَلِّصْنَا مِنَ النَّارِ ۲۳

يَا اَحْكَمَ الْحَاكِمِينَ ۞

يَا اَعْدَلَ الْعَادِلِينَ ۞

يَا اَصْدَقَ الصَّادِقِينَ ۞

يَا اَظْهَرَ الظَّاهِرِينَ ۞

يَا اَطْهَرَ الطَّاهِرِينَ ۞

يَا اَحْسَنَ الْخَالِقِينَ ۞

يَا اَسْرَعَ الْحَاسِبِينَ ۞

يَا اَسْمَعَ السَّامِعِينَ ۞

10. O the One Who provides bounty and favor in advance before the good deeds of His servants have been performed, Who has never-ceasing bounty and favor.

All-Glorified are You; there is no deity but You!
Mercy! Mercy! Save us from the Fire!

24

1. O the Wisest of the wise,

2. O the most Just of the just,

3. O the Truest of the truthful,

4. O the Most Manifest of the manifest,

5. O the Purest of the pure,

6. O He Who creates in the most perfect fashion,

7. O the Most Swift of those who judge,

8. O the Best of hearers,

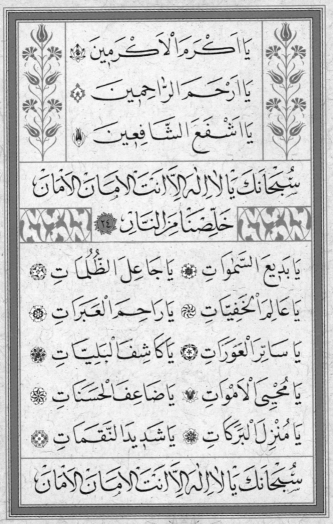

يَا اَكْرَمَ الْاَكْرَمِينَ ۞

يَا اَرْحَمَ الرَّاحِمِينَ ۞

يَا اَشْفَعَ الشَّافِعِينَ ۞

سُبْحَانَكَ يَا لَا اِلٰهَ اِلَّا اَنْتَ الْاَمَانَ الْاَمَانَ

خَلِّصْنَا مِنَ النَّارِ ۞٢٤

يَا بَدِيعَ السَّمٰوَاتِ ۞ يَا جَاعِلَ الظُّلُمَاتِ ۞

يَا عَالِمَ الْخَفِيَّاتِ ۞ يَا رَاحِمَ الْعَبَرَاتِ ۞

يَا سَاتِرَ الْعَوْرَاتِ ۞ يَا كَاشِفَ الْبَلِيَّاتِ ۞

يَا مُحْيِيَ الْاَمْوَاتِ ۞ يَا مُضَاعِفَ الْحَسَنَاتِ ۞

يَا مُنْزِلَ الْبَرَكَاتِ ۞ يَا شَدِيدَ النَّقِمَاتِ ۞

سُبْحَانَكَ يَا لَا اِلٰهَ اِلَّا اَنْتَ الْاَمَانَ الْاَمَانَ

9. O the Most Munificent of the munificent,

10. O the Most Compassionate of the compassionate,

11. O the Best of intercessors,

All-Glorified are You; there is no deity but You!
Mercy! Mercy! Save us from the Fire!

25

1. O the Originator of the heavens Who has nothing preceding Him to imitate,

2. O He Who has brought veils of darkness into being,

3. O the All-Knowing of all secrets,

4. O He Who is compassionate to those who suffer in agony and shed tears,

5. O He Who veils shameful and ugly things,

6. O He Who removes distress and calamity,

7. O He Who resurrects the dead,

8. O He Who rewards generously in return for the good deeds of His servants,

9. O He Who pours down abundance,

10. O He Who is very severe in punishing those who deserve punishment,

خَلِّصْنَا مِنَ النَّارِ ﴿٢٥﴾

وَأَسْأَلُكَ بِأَسْمَائِكَ يَا مُصَوِّرُ ۞ يَا مُقَدِّرُ ۞

يَا مُطَهِّرُ ۞ يَا مُنَوِّرُ ۞ يَا مُقَدِّمُ ۞ يَا مُؤَخِّرُ ۞

يَا مُيَسِّرُ ۞ يَا مُنْذِرُ ۞ يَا مُبَشِّرُ ۞ يَا مُدَبِّرُ ۞

سُبْحَانَكَ يَا لَا إِلَهَ إِلَّا أَنْتَ الْأَمَانَ الْأَمَانَ

خَلِّصْنَا مِنَ النَّارِ ﴿٢٦﴾

يَا رَبَّ الْبَيْتِ الْحَرَامِ ۞

يَا رَبَّ الشَّهْرِ الْحَرَامِ ۞

يَا رَبَّ الْمَسْجِدِ الْحَرَامِ ۞

يَا رَبَّ الْبَلَدِ الْحَرَامِ ۞

يَا رَبَّ الرُّكْنِ وَالْمَقَامِ ۞

All-Glorified are You; there is no deity but You!
Mercy! Mercy! Save us from the Fire!

26

I entreat You by Your Names:

1. O the All-Fashioning, (Who creates in any form He wills,)
2. O the All-Determining, (Who gives everything a unique life and nature, and determines a goal for each creature),
3. O the All-Purifying,
4. O the All-Illuminating,
5. O the All-Promoting, (Who promotes whomever He wills, with regard to honor, rank, place or time,)
6. O the All-Delaying, (Who delays what He wills, how He wills),
7. O the All-Expediting, (Who makes the difficult easy and Who gives goodness or evil to those who seek them,)
8. O the All-Warning, (Who protects His servants from evil consequences,)
9. O the Herald of glad tidings,
10. O the All-Governing,

All-Glorified are You; there is no deity but You!
Mercy! Mercy! Save us from the Fire!

27

1. O the Lord of al-Bayt al-Haram (the Sacred House: the Ka'ba,)
2. O the Lord of ash-Shahr al-Haram (the sacred, inviolable months,)
3. O the Lord of al-Masjid al-Haram (the Sacred, Inviolable Mosque in Makka,)
4. O the Lord of al-Balad al-Haram (the holy city: Makka),
5. O the Lord of ar-Rukn wa'l-Maqam (the corners of the Ka'ba and the Station of Abraham near the Ka'ba,)

يَا رَبَّ الْمَشْعَرِ الْحَرَامِ ۞

يَا رَبَّ الْحِلِّ وَالْحَرَمِ ۞

يَا رَبَّ النُّورِ وَالظَّلَامِ ۞

يَا رَبَّ التَّحِيَّةِ وَالسَّلَامِ ۞

يَا رَبَّ الْجَلَالِ وَالْإِكْرَامِ ۞

سُبْحَانَكَ يَا لَا إِلٰهَ إِلَّا أَنْتَ الْأَمَانَ الْأَمَانَ

خَلِّصْنَا مِنَ النَّارِ ۞

يَا عِمَادَ مَنْ لَا عِمَادَ لَهُ ۞

يَا سَنَدَ مَنْ لَا سَنَدَ لَهُ ۞

يَا ذُخْرَ مَنْ لَا ذُخْرَ لَهُ ۞

يَا غِيَاثَ مَنْ لَا غِيَاثَ لَهُ ۞

٣٦

6. O the Lord of al-Mash'ar al-Haram (the sacred hill in Muzdalifa,)

7. O the Lord of al-Hill and al-Haram (the free areas and the sanctified area in the Hijaz region),

8. O the Lord of the light and the darkness (day and night),

9. O He Who is the only source of security and peace,

10. O the Lord of Majesty and Graciousness,

All-Glorified are You; there is no deity but You!
Mercy! Mercy! Save us from the Fire!

28

1. O He Who is the Support of those who lack support,

2. O He Who is the Prop of those who lack a prop,

3. O He Who is the Provider of those who lack provisions,

4. O He Who is the Helper of those who lack a helper,

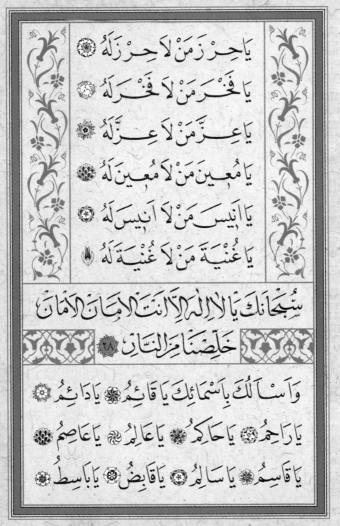

يَا حِرْزَ مَنْ لَا حِرْزَ لَهُ ۞

يَا فَخْرَ مَنْ لَا فَخْرَ لَهُ ۞

يَا عِزَّ مَنْ لَا عِزَّ لَهُ ۞

يَا مُعِينَ مَنْ لَا مُعِينَ لَهُ ۞

يَا أَنِيسَ مَنْ لَا أَنِيسَ لَهُ ۞

يَا غُنْيَةَ مَنْ لَا غُنْيَةَ لَهُ ۞

سُبْحَانَكَ يَا لَا إِلَهَ إِلَّا أَنْتَ الْأَمَانَ الْأَمَانَ خَلِّصْنَا مِنَ النَّارِ ۞ (٢٨)

وَأَسْأَلُكَ بِأَسْمَائِكَ يَا قَائِمُ ۞ يَا دَائِمُ ۞

يَا رَاحِمُ ۞ يَا حَاكِمُ ۞ يَا عَالِمُ ۞ يَا عَاصِمُ ۞

يَا قَاسِمُ ۞ يَا سَالِمُ ۞ يَا قَابِضُ ۞ يَا بَاسِطُ ۞

5. O He Who is the Refuge of those who lack refuge,
6. O He Who is the Pride of those who have nothing to be proud of,
7. O He Who is the Source of honor and might for those without honor or might,
8. O He Who is the Assistant of those who lack assistance,
9. O He Who is the Companion of those who lack a companion,
10. O He Who is the Infinite wealth of those who lack wealth,

All-Glorified are You; there is no deity but You!
Mercy! Mercy! Save us from the Fire!

29

I ask You by Your Names:

1. O the All-Enduring, (by Whom all endure),
2. O the All-Perpetual (Who has neither a beginning nor an end),
3. O the All-Compassionate, (Who shows special mercy for each creature),
4. O the All-Ruling and Judging,
5. O the All-Knowing,
6. O the All-Safeguarding,
7. O the All-Apportioning and Distinguishing, (Who apportions everything with justice,)
8. O the All-Sound, (Who is free from all shame, fault, and deficiencies,)
9. O the All-Constricting, (Who contracts hearts and Who lessens the provision of whom He wills,)
10. O the All-Expanding, (Who expands hearts and Who increases whom He wills in provision,)

سُبْحَانَكَ يَا لَا إِلَهَ إِلَّا أَنْتَ الْأَمَانَ الْأَمَانَ

خَلِّصْنَا مِنَ النَّارِ ﴿٢٩﴾

يَا عَاصِمَ مَنِ اسْتَعْصَمَهُ ۞

يَا رَاحِمَ مَنِ اسْتَرْحَمَهُ ۞

يَا نَاصِرَ مَنِ اسْتَنْصَرَهُ ۞

يَا حَافِظَ مَنِ اسْتَحْفَظَهُ ۞

يَا مُكْرِمَ مَنِ اسْتَكْرَمَهُ ۞

يَا مُرْشِدَ مَنِ اسْتَرْشَدَهُ ۞

يَا مُعِينَ مَنِ اسْتَعَانَهُ ۞

يَا مُغِيثَ مَنِ اسْتَغَاثَهُ ۞

يَا صَرِيخَ مَنِ اسْتَصْرَخَهُ ۞

All-Glorified are You; there is no deity but You!
Mercy! Mercy! Save us from the Fire!

30

1. O He Who guards those who take refuge in Him,
2. O He Who shows mercy on those who seek His mercy,
3. O He Who helps those who ask for His help,
4. O He Who preserves those who ask for His preservation,
5. O He Who blesses those who ask for His blessings
6. O He Who guides to the right path those who ask for guidance,
7. O He Who aids those who ask for His aid,
8. O He Who assists those who expect His assistance,
9. O He Who hears the cry of those who cry out,

يَا غَافِرَ مَنِ اسْتَغْفَرَهُ ۞

سُبْحَانَكَ يَا لَا إِلٰهَ إِلَّا أَنْتَ الْأَمَانَ الْأَمَانَ

خَلِّصْنَا مِنَ النَّارِ ۳۰

يَا كَرِيمَ الصَّفْحِ ۞ يَا عَظِيمَ الْمَنِّ

يَا كَثِيرَ الْخَيْرِ ۞ يَا قَدِيمَ الْفَضْلِ

يَا لَطِيفَ الصُّنْعِ ۞ يَا دَائِمَ اللُّطْفِ

يَا نَافِسَ الْكَرْبِ ۞ يَا كَاشِفَ الضُّرِّ

يَا مَالِكَ الْمُلْكِ ۞ يَا قَاضِيًا بِالْحَقِّ

سُبْحَانَكَ يَا لَا إِلٰهَ إِلَّا أَنْتَ الْأَمَانَ الْأَمَانَ

أَجِرْنَا مِنَ النَّارِ ۳۱

يَا عَزِيزًا لَا يُضَامُ ۞ يَا لَطِيفًا لَا يُرَامُ ۞

10. O He Who forgives those who ask Him for forgiveness,

All-Glorified are You; there is no deity but You!
Mercy! Mercy! Save us from the Fire!

31

1. O the One of generous pardon and tolerance,

2. O the One of supreme blessing,

3. O the One of abundant good,

4. O the One of pre-eternal grace,

5. O the One of delicate making,

6. O the One of everlasting bounty,

7. O the Eliminator of troubles,

8. O the Remover of harmful things,

9. O the Owner of sovereignty and rule,

10. O He Who judges rightly and justly,

All-Glorified are You; there is no deity but You!
Mercy! Mercy! Protect us from the Fire!

32

1. O the Invincible, All-Glorious with irresistible might,

2. O the All-Subtle, All-Gracious, Whose very Essence cannot be known,

يَا رَقِيبًا لَا يَنَامُ ۞ يَا قَائِمًا لَا يَفُوتُ ۞

يَا حَيًّا لَا يَمُوتُ ۞ يَا مَلِكًا لَا يَزُولُ ۞

يَا بَاقِيًا لَا يَفْنَى ۞ يَا عَالِمًا لَا يَجْهَلُ ۞

يَا صَمَدًا لَا يُطْعَمُ ۞ يَا قَوِيًّا لَا يَضْعُفُ ۞

سُبْحَانَكَ يَا لَا إِلٰهَ إِلَّا أَنْتَ الْأَمَانَ الْأَمَانَ

أَجِرْنَا مِنَ النَّارِ ۞ ٣٢

وَأَسْأَلُكَ بِأَسْمَائِكَ يَا وَاحِدُ ۞ يَا وَاجِدُ ۞

يَا شَاهِدُ ۞ يَا مَاجِدُ ۞ يَا رَاشِدُ ۞ يَا بَاعِثُ ۞

يَا وَارِثُ ۞ يَا ضَارُّ ۞ يَا نَافِعُ ۞ يَا هَادِي ۞

سُبْحَانَكَ يَا لَا إِلٰهَ إِلَّا أَنْتَ الْأَمَانَ الْأَمَانَ

أَجِرْنَا مِنَ النَّارِ ۞ ٣٣

3. O the All-Watchful, Who never sleeps,
4. O the All-Enduring, Who will never cease to be,
5. O the All-Living, Who will never die,
6. O the All-Sovereign, Who will never perish,
7. O the All-Permanent, Who will never pass away,
8. O the All-Knowing, Who is untainted by ignorance,
9. O the Eternally Besought-of-all, Who never needs food or drink,
10. O the All-Strong, Who cannot be debilitated,

All-Glorified are You; there is no deity but You!
Mercy! Mercy! Protect us from the Fire!

33

I entreat You by Your Names:

1. O the All-One (Who has no partners and equals, Whose Names are manifested upon the whole),
2. O the Ever-Present and All-Finding,
3. O the All-Witnessing, (from Whom nothing can be hidden,)
4. O the All-Sublime, (Who has infinite glory,)
5. O the All-Right, (Who is absolutely right in all His deeds and decrees,)
6. O the All-Restoring and Reviving, (Who sends Messengers to revive people spiritually, and Who will restore life to the dead,)
7. O the All-Inheriting, (Who survives all beings and inherits them,)
8. O the Causer of harm, (Whose harm nobody can prevent if He wills to harm someone,)
9. O the All-Favoring and Giver of benefits,
10. O the All-Guiding, (Who creates and grants guidance,)

All-Glorified are You; there is no deity but You!
Mercy! Mercy! Protect us from the Fire!

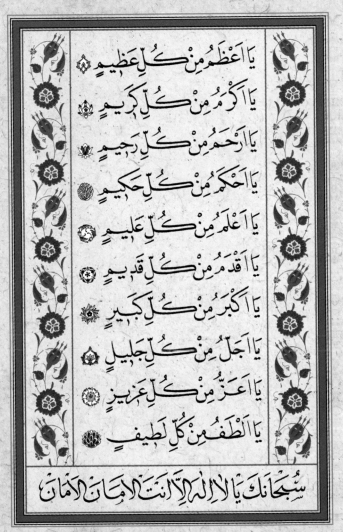

يَا اَعْظَمَ مِنْ كُلِّ عَظِيمٍ ۞

يَا اَكْرَمَ مِنْ كُلِّ كَرِيمٍ ۞

يَا اَرْحَمَ مِنْ كُلِّ رَحِيمٍ ۞

يَا اَحْكَمَ مِنْ كُلِّ حَكِيمٍ ۞

يَا اَعْلَمَ مِنْ كُلِّ عَلِيمٍ ۞

يَا اَقْدَمَ مِنْ كُلِّ قَدِيمٍ ۞

يَا اَكْبَرَ مِنْ كُلِّ كَبِيرٍ ۞

يَا اَجَلَّ مِنْ كُلِّ جَلِيلٍ ۞

يَا اَعَزَّ مِنْ كُلِّ عَزِيزٍ ۞

يَا اَلْطَفَ مِنْ كُلِّ لَطِيفٍ ۞

سُبْحَانَكَ يَا لَا اِلٰهَ اِلَّا اَنْتَ الْاَمَانَ الْاَمَانَ

34

1. O He Who is infinitely more supreme than any supreme being,

2. O He Who is infinitely more munificent than any munificent being,

3. O He Who is infinitely more compassionate than any compassionate being,

4. O He Who is infinitely wiser than any wise being,

5. O He Who is infinitely more knowledgeable than any knowledgeable being,

6. O He Who pre-eternally precedes anything that has existed from the earliest times,

7. O He Who is infinitely greater than any great being,

8. O He Who is infinitely more majestic than any majestic being,

9. O He Who is infinitely more glorious and mightier than any glorious and mighty being,

10. O He Who is infinitely more subtle and gracious than any subtle and gracious being,

All-Glorified are You; there is no deity but You!
Mercy! Mercy! Protect us from the Fire!

يَا مَنْ هُوَ فِى عَهْدِهِ وَفِىٌّ ۝

يَا مَنْ هُوَ فِى وَفَائِهِ قَوِىٌّ ۝

يَا مَنْ هُوَ فِى قُوَّتِهِ عَلِىٌّ ۝

يَا مَنْ هُوَ فِى عُلُوِّهِ قَرِيبٌ ۝

يَا مَنْ هُوَ فِى قُرْبِهِ لَطِيفٌ ۝

يَا مَنْ هُوَ فِى لُطْفِهِ شَرِيفٌ ۝

يَا مَنْ هُوَ فِى شَرَفِهِ عَزِيزٌ ۝

يَا مَنْ هُوَ فِى عِزَّتِهِ عَظِيمٌ ۝

يَا مَنْ هُوَ فِى عَظَمَتِهِ مَجِيدٌ ۝

يَا مَنْ هُوَ فِى مَجْدِهِ حَمِيدٌ ۝

35

1. O He Who is all-faithful in His covenant, in keeping His promise,

2. O He Who is all-strong and powerful in fulfilling what He promises,

3. O He Who is all-exalted in His Strength,

4. O He Who is all-near to everything in His Exaltedness,

5. O He Who is all-subtle in His Nearness,

6. O He Who is all-noble in His Subtlety,

7. O He Who is all-glorious and mighty in His Nobility,

8. O He Who is all-supreme in His Glory and Might,

9. O He Who is all-sublime in His Supremeness,

10. O He Who is all-praiseworthy in His Sublimity,

سُبْحَانَكَ يَا اللهُ لَا إِلَهَ إِلَّا أَنْتَ الْأَمَانَ الْأَمَانَ

أَجِرْنَا مِنَ النَّارِ ٣٥

يَا مَنْ هُوَ كُلُّ شَيْءٍ خَاضِعٌ لَهُ ۞

يَا مَنْ هُوَ كُلُّ شَيْءٍ كَائِنٌ لَهُ ۞

يَا مَنْ هُوَ كُلُّ شَيْءٍ مَوْجُودٌ لَهُ ۞

يَا مَنْ هُوَ كُلُّ شَيْءٍ مُنِيبٌ لَهُ ۞

يَا مَنْ هُوَ كُلُّ شَيْءٍ خَائِفٌ مِنْهُ ۞

يَا مَنْ هُوَ كُلُّ شَيْءٍ مُسَبِّحٌ لَهُ ۞

يَا مَنْ هُوَ كُلُّ شَيْءٍ قَائِمٌ بِهِ ۞

يَا مَنْ هُوَ كُلُّ شَيْءٍ خَاشِعٌ لَهُ ۞

يَا مَنْ هُوَ كُلُّ شَيْءٍ صَائِرٌ إِلَيْهِ ۞

All-Glorified are You; there is no deity but You!
Mercy! Mercy! Protect us from the Fire!

36

1. O He to Whom all things submit in complete obedience,

2. O He for Whom all things come into being,

3. O He for Whom all things exist,

4. O He toward Whom all things turn (in supplication),

5. O He Whom all things fear,

6. O He Whom all things glorify,

7. O He by Whom all things subsist and last,

8. O He in awe of Whom all things humbly obey,

9. O He to Whom all things are bound to return,

يَا مَنْ هُوَ كُلُّ شَيْءٍ هَالِكٌ إِلَّا وَجْهَهُ ۞

سُبْحَانَكَ يَا لَا إِلَٰهَ إِلَّا أَنْتَ الْأَمَانَ الْأَمَانَ

أَجِرْنَا مِنَ النَّارِ ۩۳٦

وَأَسْأَلُكَ بِأَسْمَائِكَ يَا كَافِي ۞ يَا شَافِي ۞

يَا وَافِي ۞ يَا مُعَافِي ۞ يَا عَالِي ۞ يَا دَاعِي ۞

يَا رَاضِي ۞ يَا قَاضِي ۞ يَا بَاقِي ۞ يَا هَادِي ۞

سُبْحَانَكَ يَا لَا إِلَٰهَ إِلَّا أَنْتَ الْأَمَانَ الْأَمَانَ

أَجِرْنَا مِنَ النَّارِ ۩۳۷

يَا مَنْ لَا مَفَرَّ إِلَّا إِلَيْهِ ۞

يَا مَنْ لَا مَفْزَعَ إِلَّا إِلَيْهِ ۞

يَا مَنْ لَا مَلْجَأَ إِلَّا إِلَيْهِ ۞

10. O He Whose Being is solely free from perishing,

All-Glorified are You; there is no deity but You!
Mercy! Mercy! Protect us from the Fire!

37

I entreat You by Your Names:

1. O the All-Sufficient One, (Who fulfills all the needs of His creatures and Who suffices for them,)
2. O the All-Healing, (Who cures all physical and spiritual diseases,)
3. O the All-Reliable, (Who is faithful to His promise and Who attends to all the needs and requests of His creatures with wisdom,)
4. O the Bestower of well-being (against all physical and spiritual diseases,)
5. O the All-High, (Who has superiority over His creatures,)
6. O the All-Inviting, (Who calls His servants to whatever is good and beneficial and Who calls them to Heaven,)
7. O He Who is all-pleased (with good deeds and His good servants,)
8. O the Supreme Judge and Executing, (Who meets the needs of creatures and Who rules with justice and wisdom,)
9. O the All-Permanent,
10. O the All-Guiding,

All-Glorified are You; there is no deity but You!
Mercy! Mercy! Protect us from the Fire!

38

1. O He Who is the only one in whom shelter can be sought,
2. O He Who is the only one to whom we can resort,
3. O He Who is the only one in whom refuge can be taken,

يَا مَنْ لَا يُتَوَكَّلُ إِلَّا عَلَيْهِ ۞

يَا مَنْ لَا مَقْصِدَ إِلَّا إِلَيْهِ ۞

يَا مَنْ لَا مَنْجَأَ إِلَّا إِلَيْهِ ۞

يَا مَنْ لَا يُرْغَبُ إِلَّا إِلَيْهِ ۞

يَا مَنْ لَا يُعْبَدُ إِلَّا إِيَّاهُ ۞

يَا مَنْ لَا يُسْتَعَانُ إِلَّا مِنْهُ ۞

يَا مَنْ لَا حَوْلَ وَلَا قُوَّةَ إِلَّا بِهِ ۞

سُبْحَانَكَ يَا لَا إِلٰهَ إِلَّا أَنْتَ الْأَمَانَ الْأَمَانَ
أَجِرْنَا مِنَ النَّارِ ۞٢٨

يَا خَيْرَ الْمَرْهُوبِينَ ۞ يَا خَيْرَ الْمَطْلُوبِينَ ۞

يَا خَيْرَ الْمَرْغُوبِينَ ۞ يَا خَيْرَ الْمَسْئُولِينَ ۞

4. O He Who is the only one in whom we can trust,

5. O He Who is the only one who must be sought,

6. O He Who is the only one in whom the way to deliverance ends,

7. O He Who is the only one to be sought and demanded,

8. O He Who is the only one to be worshipped,

9. O He Who is the only one to be asked for help,

10. O He who is the only one with absolute force and power,

All-Glorified are You; there is no deity but You!
Mercy! Mercy! Protect us from the Fire!

39

1. O the Best of those who are feared,

2. O the Best of those who are longed for,

3. O the Best of those who are sought after,

4. O the Best of those to whom requests are made,

يَا خَيْرَ الْمَقْصُودِينَ 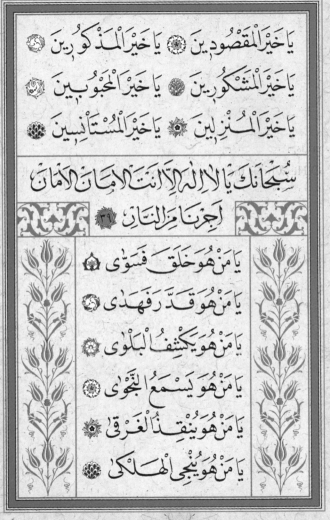 يَا خَيْرَ الْمَذْكُورِينَ ۞

يَا خَيْرَ الْمَشْكُورِينَ ۞ يَا خَيْرَ الْمَحْبُوبِينَ ۞

يَا خَيْرَ الْمُنْزِلِينَ ۞ يَا خَيْرَ الْمُسْتَأْنِسِينَ ۞

سُبْحَانَكَ يَا لَا إِلَهَ إِلَّا أَنْتَ الْأَمَانَ الْأَمَانَ

أَجِرْنَا مِنَ النَّارِ ۞

يَا مَنْ هُوَ خَلَقَ فَسَوَّى ۞

يَا مَنْ هُوَ قَدَّرَ فَهَدَى ۞

يَا مَنْ هُوَ يَكْشِفُ الْبَلْوَى ۞

يَا مَنْ هُوَ يَسْمَعُ النَّجْوَى ۞

يَا مَنْ هُوَ يُنْقِذُ الْغَرْقَى ۞

يَا مَنْ هُوَ يُنْجِي الْهَلْكَى ۞

5. O the Best of aims and objectives,

6. O the Best of those who are remembered and mentioned,

7. O the Best of those who are thanked and praised,

8. O the Best of those who are loved,

9. O the Best of hosts,

10. O the Best of those who are befriended,

All-Glorified are You; there is no deity but You!
Mercy! Mercy! Protect us from the Fire!

40

1. O He Who creates and fashions in due proportion,

2. O He Who determines (a particular life, nature, and goal for each creature), and guides (it toward the fulfillment of that goal),

3. O We Who removes troubles,

4. O He Who hears secret counsels and conversations,

5. O He Who rescues those who are drawn into physical and spiritual disasters and calamities,

6. O He Who saves those who are on the verge of destruction,

يَا مَنْ هُوَ يَشْفِى الْمَرْضَى ۞

۞ يَا مَنْ هُوَ أَمَاتَ وَأَحْيَا

يَا مَنْ هُوَ أَضْحَكَ وَأَبْكَى ۞

۞ يَا مَنْ هُوَ أَضَلَّ وَأَهْدَى

سُبْحَانَكَ يَا لَا إِلَهَ إِلَّا أَنْتَ الْأَمَانَ الْأَمَانَ
أَجِرْنَا مِنَ النَّارِ ﴿٤۰﴾

وَأَسْأَلُكَ بِأَسْمَائِكَ يَا غَافِرُ ۞ يَا سَاتِرُ

يَا قَاهِرُ ۞ يَا قَادِرُ ۞ يَا نَاظِرُ ۞ يَا فَاطِرُ

يَا شَاكِرُ ۞ يَا ذَاكِرُ ۞ يَا نَاصِرُ ۞ يَا جَابِرُ ۞

سُبْحَانَكَ يَا لَا إِلَهَ إِلَّا أَنْتَ الْأَمَانَ الْأَمَانَ
أَجِرْنَا مِنَ النَّارِ ﴿٤١﴾

٣٧

7. O He Who cures those who are physically or spiritually ill,
8. O He Who causes to die and revives,
9. O He Who causes to rejoice, laugh, and to weep,
10. O He Who leads astray and guides to the Straight Path,

All-Glorified are You; there is no deity but You!
Mercy! Mercy! Protect us from the Fire!

41

I entreat You by Your Names:

1. O the All-Forgiving,
2. O the All-Veiling, (Who veils the shame and faults of His servants),
3. O the All-Overwhelming, (Who prevails over the whole universe with His absolute Rule and Power),
4. O the All-Powerful,
5. O the All-Viewing,
6. O the All-Originator, (Who originates each thing with a unique individuality,)
7. O the All-Responsive (to the gratitude of His creatures)
8. O the All-Remembering and Mentioning, (Who remembers and mentions in high assemblies those who remember and mention Him,)
9. O the All-Helping and Giver of victory,
10. O the All-Compelling,

All-Glorified are You; there is no deity but You!
Mercy! Mercy! Protect us from the Fire!

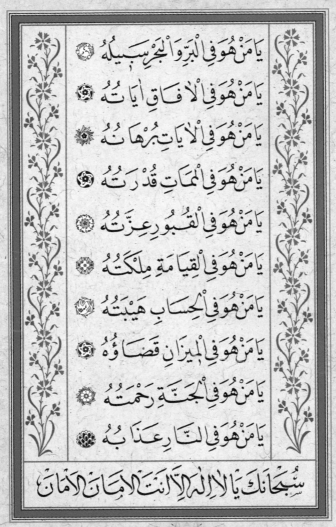

يَا مَنْ هُوَ فِي الْبَرِّ وَالْبَحْرِ سَبِيلُهُ ۞

يَا مَنْ هُوَ فِي الْآفَاقِ آيَاتُهُ ۞

يَا مَنْ هُوَ فِي الْآيَاتِ بُرْهَانُهُ ۞

يَا مَنْ هُوَ فِي الْمَمَاتِ قُدْرَتُهُ ۞

يَا مَنْ هُوَ فِي الْقُبُورِ عِزَّتُهُ ۞

يَا مَنْ هُوَ فِي الْقِيَامَةِ مِلْكَتُهُ ۞

يَا مَنْ هُوَ فِي الْحِسَابِ هَيْبَتُهُ ۞

يَا مَنْ هُوَ فِي الْمِيزَانِ قَضَاؤُهُ ۞

يَا مَنْ هُوَ فِي الْجَنَّةِ رَحْمَتُهُ ۞

يَا مَنْ هُوَ فِي النَّارِ عَذَابُهُ ۞

سُبْحَانَكَ يَا لَا إِلَهَ إِلَّا أَنْتَ الْأَمَانَ الْأَمَانَ

42

1. O He Who has ways (which He has created) over land and sea (by which His servants may travel),

2. O He Who has signs (for His Existence and Oneness, and for His Attributes) throughout the universe,

3. O He in Whose signs there is evidence of His existence,

4. O He Who manifests His Power through death,

5. O He Who has His Glory and Might in the grave,

6. O He Who has Authority and Sovereignty in the Resurrection,

7. O He Who has Grandeur and Majesty in the Final Reckoning,

8. O He Who has Judgment and Execution in the Balance,

9. O He Who has Mercy in Paradise,

10. O He Who has punishment in the Fire,

All-Glorified are You; there is no deity but You!
Mercy! Mercy! Protect us from the Fire!

يَا مَنْ هُوَ إِلَيْهِ يَهْرُبُ الْخَائِفُونَ ۞

يَا مَنْ هُوَ إِلَيْهِ يَفْزَعُ الْمُذْنِبُونَ ۞

يَا مَنْ هُوَ إِلَيْهِ يَقْصِدُ الْمُنِيبُونَ ۞

يَا مَنْ هُوَ إِلَيْهِ يَلْجَأُ الْعَاصُونَ ۞

يَا مَنْ هُوَ إِلَيْهِ يَرْغَبُ الزَّاهِدُونَ ۞

يَا مَنْ هُوَ فِيهِ يَطْمَعُ الْخَاطِئُونَ ۞

يَا مَنْ هُوَ يَسْتَأْنِسُ بِهِ الْمُرِيدُونَ ۞

يَا مَنْ هُوَ يَفْتَخِرُ بِهِ الْمُحْسِنُونَ ۞

يَا مَنْ هُوَ عَلَيْهِ يَتَوَكَّلُ الْمُتَوَكِّلُونَ ۞

يَا مَنْ هُوَ يَسْكُنُ بِهِ الْمُوقِنُونَ ۞

43

1. O He to Whom the frightened flee,

2. O He in Whom sinners take shelter,

3. O He to Whom the repentant turn,

4. O He with Whom the rebellious seek refuge,

5. O He Whom the pious seek,

6. O He of Whom the guilty are hopeful,

7. O He in Whom those who are seeking find friendship,

8. O He of Whom the godly and virtuous are proud,

9. O He in Whom trust is placed,

10. O He with Whom those with certainty of belief can find inner-peace,

سُبْحَانَكَ يَا لَا إِلٰهَ إِلَّا أَنْتَ الْأَمَانَ الْأَمَانَ

أَجِرْنَا مِنَ النَّارِ ۞

يَا أَقْرَبَ مِنْ كُلِّ قَرِيبٍ ۞

يَا أَحَبَّ مِنْ كُلِّ حَبِيبٍ ۞

يَا أَعْظَمَ مِنْ كُلِّ عَظِيمٍ ۞

يَا أَعَزَّ مِنْ كُلِّ عَزِيزٍ ۞

يَا أَقْوٰى مِنْ كُلِّ قَوِيٍّ ۞

يَا أَغْنٰى مِنْ كُلِّ غَنِيٍّ ۞

يَا أَجْوَدَ مِنْ كُلِّ جَوَادٍ ۞

يَا أَرْأَفَ مِنْ كُلِّ رَؤُوفٍ ۞

يَا أَرْحَمَ مِنْ كُلِّ رَحِيمٍ ۞

All-Glorified are You; there is no deity but You!
Mercy! Mercy! Protect us from the Fire!

44

1. O He Who is infinitely nearer than anyone near,
2. O He Who is infinitely more beloved than anyone beloved,
3. O He Who is infinitely more supreme than anyone supreme,
4. O He Who is infinitely more glorious and mighty than anyone of glory and might,
5. O He Who is infinitely stronger than anyone strong,
6. O He Who is infinitely wealthier than anyone wealthy,
7. O He Who is infinitely more generous than anyone generous,
8. O He Who is infinitely more affectionate than anyone affectionate,
9. O He Who is infinitely more compassionate than anyone compassionate,

يَا أَجَلَّ مِنْ كُلِّ جَلِيلٍ ۞

سُبْحَانَكَ يَا لَا إِلَهَ إِلَّا أَنْتَ الْأَمَانَ الْأَمَانَ
أَجِرْنَا مِنَ النَّارِ ۞٤٤

وَأَسْأَلُكَ بِأَسْمَائِكَ يَا قَرِيبُ ۞ يَا رَقِيبُ ۞
يَا حَبِيبُ ۞ يَا مُجِيبُ ۞ يَا حَسِيبُ ۞ يَا طَبِيبُ ۞
يَا بَصِيرُ ۞ يَا خَبِيرُ ۞ يَا مُنِيرُ ۞ يَا مُبِينُ ۞

سُبْحَانَكَ يَا لَا إِلَهَ إِلَّا أَنْتَ الْأَمَانَ الْأَمَانَ
أَجِرْنَا مِنَ النَّارِ ۞٤٥

يَا غَالِبًا غَيْرَ مَغْلُوبٍ ۞
يَا صَانِعًا غَيْرَ مَصْنُوعٍ ۞
يَا خَالِقًا غَيْرَ مَخْلُوقٍ ۞

٤١

10. O He Who is infinitely more majestic than anyone majestic,

All-Glorified are You; there is no deity but You!
Mercy! Mercy! Protect us from the Fire!

45

I entreat You by Your Names:

1. O the All-Near, (Who is nearer to everything than itself),
2. O the All-Watchful, (Who never neglects any of His creatures,)
3. O the All-Beloved, (Who causes His servants to love Him and Who loves His servants,)
4. O the All-Answering, (Who answers the prayers and requests of His creatures in the wisest and most proper way,)
5. O the All-Sufficing as One Who reckons and settles the accounts (of His servants),
6. O the All-Curing, (Who provides cure for all diseases),
7. O the All-Seeing,
8. O the All-Aware,
9. O the All-Illuminating,
10. O the All-Evident (from Whom nothing is hidden and Who makes all truth manifest),

All-Glorified are You; there is no deity but You!
Mercy! Mercy! Protect us from the Fire!

46

1. O the All-Victorious Who is never defeated,
2. O the Maker (with perfect art) Who has not been made,
3. O the Creator Who has never been created,

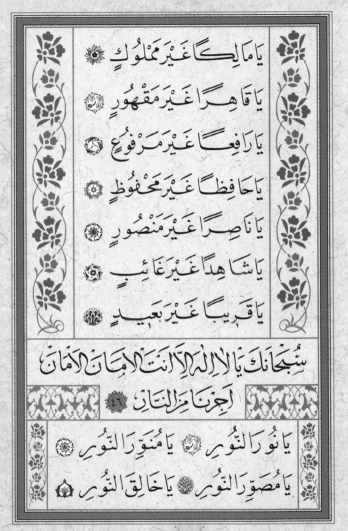

يَا مَالِكًا غَيْرَ مَمْلُوكٍ ۞

يَا قَاهِرًا غَيْرَ مَقْهُورٍ ۞

يَا رَافِعًا غَيْرَ مَرْفُوعٍ ۞

يَا حَافِظًا غَيْرَ مَحْفُوظٍ ۞

يَا نَاصِرًا غَيْرَ مَنْصُورٍ ۞

يَا شَاهِدًا غَيْرَ غَائِبٍ ۞

يَا قَرِيبًا غَيْرَ بَعِيدٍ ۞

سُبْحَانَكَ يَا لَا إِلَهَ إِلَّا أَنْتَ الْأَمَانَ الْأَمَانَ
أَجِرْنَا مِنَ النَّارِ ۞٤٦

يَا نُورَ النُّورِ ۞ يَا مُنَوِّرَ النُّورِ ۞
يَا مُصَوِّرَ النُّورِ ۞ يَا خَالِقَ النُّورِ ۞

4. O the Master Who has never been owned,

5. O the All-Overwhelming Who has never been ruled or overwhelmed,

6. O the All-Exalting Who has never been made exalted by others.

7. O the All-Preserving Who has never been preserved,

8. O the All-Helping Who has never been helped,

9. O the All-Witnessing and Ever-Present Who has never been distant or unaware,

10. O the All-Near Who has never been remote,

All-Glorified are You; there is no deity but You!
Mercy! Mercy! Protect us from the Fire!

47

1. O the Light of all light,

2. O the Illuminator of light,

3. O He Who gives form and image to light,

4. O the Creator of light,

يَا مُقَدِّرَ النُّورِ ۞ يَا مُدَبِّرَ النُّورِ ۞

يَا نُورًا قَبْلَ كُلِّ نُورٍ ۞ يَا نُورًا بَعْدَ كُلِّ نُورٍ ۞

يَا نُورًا فَوْقَ كُلِّ نُورٍ ۞ يَا نُورًا لَيْسَ مِثْلَهُ نُورٌ ۞

سُبْحَانَكَ يَا لَا إِلَهَ إِلَّا أَنْتَ الْأَمَانَ الْأَمَانَ

أَجِرْنَا مِنَ النَّارِ ۞

يَا مَنْ عَطَاؤُهُ شَرِيفٌ ۞ يَا مَنْ فِعْلُهُ لَطِيفٌ ۞

يَا مَنْ لُطْفُهُ مُقِيمٌ ۞ يَا مَنْ إِحْسَانُهُ قَدِيمٌ ۞

يَا مَنْ قَوْلُهُ حَقٌّ ۞ يَا مَنْ وَعْدُهُ صِدْقٌ ۞

يَا مَنْ عَفْوُهُ فَضْلٌ ۞ يَا مَنْ عَذَابُهُ عَدْلٌ ۞

يَا مَنْ ذِكْرُهُ حُلْوٌ ۞ يَا مَنْ أُنْسُهُ لَذِيذٌ ۞

سُبْحَانَكَ يَا لَا إِلَهَ إِلَّا أَنْتَ الْأَمَانَ الْأَمَانَ

5. O He Who determines light in certain measures,

6. O He Who administers light,

7. O the Light, Who existed before all light,

8. O the Light, Who will continue to exist when all lights have been extinguished,

9. O the Light, Who is above all light,

10. O the Light, Whom no light resembles or is like,

All-Glorified are You; there is no deity but You!
Mercy! Mercy! Protect us from the Fire!

48

1. O He Whose bestowal is noble,

2. O He Whose work is subtle and fine,

3. O He Whose favors and generosity are lasting,

4. O He Whose benevolence is eternal,

5. O He Whose word is right,

6. O He Whose promise is true,

7. O He Whose forgiveness emanates purely from His Grace,

8. O He Whose punishment is pure justice,

9. O He Whose remembrance is pleasant,

10. O He Whose nearness and friendship is a pleasure,

All-Glorified are You; there is no deity but You!
Mercy! Mercy! Protect us from the Fire!

وَأَسْأَلُكَ بِأَسْمَائِكَ يَا مَنَوْلُ ۞ يَا مُفَصِّلُ ۞

يَا مُبَدِّلُ ۞ يَا مُسَهِّلُ ۞ يَا مُذَلِّلُ ۞ يَا مُنَزِّلُ ۞

يَا مُحَوِّلُ ۞ يَا مُجَمِّلُ ۞ يَا مُكَمِّلُ ۞ يَا مُفَضِّلُ ۞

سُبْحَانَكَ يَا لَا إِلٰهَ إِلَّا أَنْتَ الْأَمَانَ الْأَمَانَ

أَجِرْنَا مِنَ النَّارِ ﴿٤٩﴾

يَا مَنْ يَرَى وَلَا يُرَى ۞

يَا مَنْ يَخْلُقُ وَلَا يُخْلَقُ ۞

يَا مَنْ يَهْدِي وَلَا يُهْدَى ۞

يَا مَنْ يُحْيِي وَلَا يُحْيَى ۞

يَا مَنْ يُطْعِمُ وَلَا يُطْعَمُ ۞

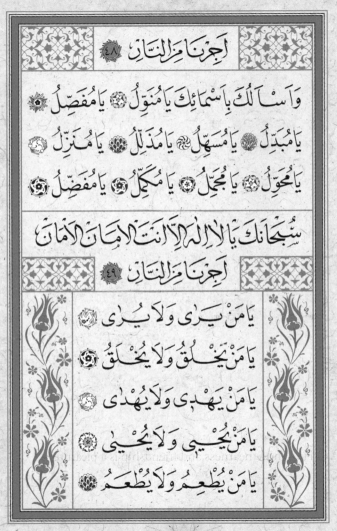

49

I entreat You by Your Names:

1. O the Granter of gifts, Who grants due blessings to His creatures,
2. O the All-Distinguishing and Explaining, Who sets His signs in detail,
3. O the All-Changing and Substituting, Who changes anything as He wills or substitutes it for another,
4. O the All-Facilitating,
5. O the All-Abasing, Who humiliates whoever He wills,
6. O the All-Conveying, Who sends down Revelations, angels, abundance, and calamity,
7. O the All-Transforming, Who changes creatures from one state to another,
8. O the All-Beautifying,
9. O the All-Perfecting,
10. O He Who renders whoever He wills superior to others,

All-Glorified are You; there is no deity but You!
Mercy! Mercy! Protect us from the Fire!

50

1. O He Who sees everything, while He is invisible,
2. O He Who creates everything, while He is not created,
3. O He Who guides everything to the straight path and shows the way, while He needs no guide,
4. O He Who gives life to everything, while He is not brought to life by anything else; He Whose life comes from Himself and is eternal,
5. O He Who nurtures everybody, while He has no need for nurture,

يَا مَنْ يُجِيرُ وَلَا يُجَارُ ۞

يَا مَنْ يَقْضِي وَلَا يُقْضَى عَلَيْهِ ۞

يَا مَنْ يَحْكُمُ وَلَا يُحْكَمُ عَلَيْهِ ۞

يَا مَنْ لَمْ يَلِدْ وَلَمْ يُولَدْ

وَلَمْ يَكُنْ لَهُ كُفُوًا أَحَدٌ ۞

سُبْحَانَكَ يَا لَا إِلَهَ إِلَّا أَنْتَ الْأَمَانَ الْأَمَانَ

أَجِرْنَا مِنَ النَّارِ ۞ ٥٠

يَا نِعْمَ الطَّبِيبُ ۞ يَا نِعْمَ الْحَبِيبُ ۞

يَا نِعْمَ الْقَرِيبُ ۞ يَا نِعْمَ الْحَسِيبُ ۞

يَا نِعْمَ الْمُجِيبُ ۞ يَا نِعْمَ الرَّقِيبُ ۞

يَا نِعْمَ الْوَكِيلُ ۞ يَا نِعْمَ الْأَنِيسُ ۞

٤٥

6. O He Who protects everything, while He has no need for protection,

7. O He Who judges and executes His judgment, while He is not to be judged,

8. O He Who rules over everything, while He is not to be ruled over,

9. O He Who does not give birth and who was not born,

10. O He to Whom nothing is equal or comparable,

All-Glorified are You; there is no deity but You!
Mercy! Mercy! Protect us from the Fire!

51

1. O He Who is unique as the All-Beloved,

2. O He Who is unique as the All-Healing,

3. O He Who is unique as the All-Reckoning,

4. O He Who is unique as the All-Near,

5. O He Who is unique as the All-Watchful,

6. O He Who is unique as the All-Answering,

7. O He Who is unique as the All-Companion,

8. O He Who is unique as One to rely on and to Whom affairs should be entrusted,

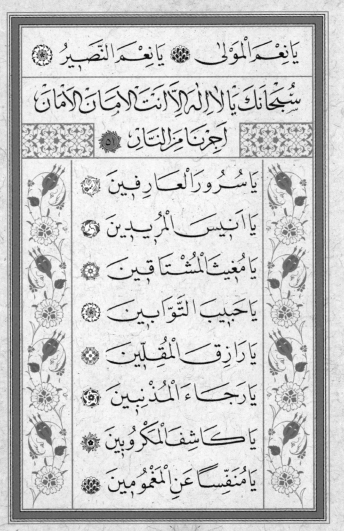

يَا نِعْمَ الْمَوْلَى ۞ يَا نِعْمَ النَّصِيرُ ۞

سُبْحَانَكَ يَا لَا إِلَهَ إِلَّا أَنْتَ الْأَمَانُ الْأَمَانُ
أَجِرْنَا مِنَ النَّارِ ۵۱

يَا سُرُورَ الْعَارِفِينَ ۞

يَا أَنِيسَ الْمُرِيدِينَ ۞

يَا مُغِيثَ الْمُشْتَاقِينَ ۞

يَا حَبِيبَ التَّوَّابِينَ ۞

يَا رَازِقَ الْمُقِلِّينَ ۞

يَا رَجَاءَ الْمُذْنِبِينَ ۞

يَا كَاشِفَ الْمَكْرُوبِينَ ۞

يَا مُنَفِّسًا عَنِ الْمَغْمُومِينَ ۞

9. O He Who is unique as the All-Protecting Owner,

10. O He Who is unique as the All-Helping,

All-Glorified are You; there is no deity but You!
Mercy! Mercy! Protect us from the Fire!

52

1. O He Who is the source of joy and happiness for those who have knowledge of Him,

2. O He Who provides friendship and peace for those who seek His good pleasure,

3. O He Who succors those who love and long for Him,

4. O He Who is the beloved of those who repent often,

5. O He Who provides for the destitute,

6. O He Who is the source of hope for sinners,

7. O He Who removes the sufferings of those in desperate straits,

8. O He Who comforts souls in times of sorrow and grief,

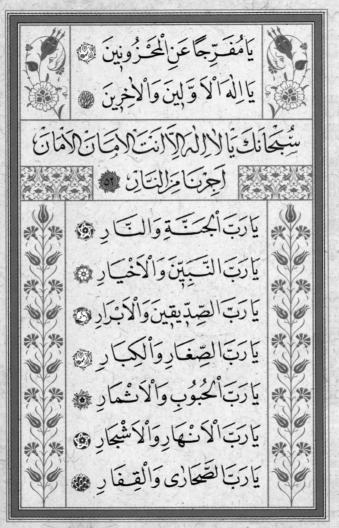

يَا مُفَرِّجًا عَنِ الْمَحْزُونِينَ ۞

يَا إِلَهَ الْأَوَّلِينَ وَالْآخِرِينَ ۞

سُبْحَانَكَ يَا لَا إِلَهَ إِلَّا أَنْتَ الْأَمَانَ الْأَمَانَ

أَجِرْنَا مِنَ النَّارِ ۝٥٢

يَا رَبَّ الْجَنَّةِ وَالنَّارِ ۞

يَا رَبَّ النَّبِيِّينَ وَالْأَخْيَارِ ۞

يَا رَبَّ الصِّدِّيقِينَ وَالْأَبْرَارِ ۞

يَا رَبَّ الصِّغَارِ وَالْكِبَارِ ۞

يَا رَبَّ الْحُبُوبِ وَالْأَثْمَارِ ۞

يَا رَبَّ الْأَنْهَارِ وَالْأَشْجَارِ ۞

يَا رَبَّ الصَّحَارَى وَالْقِفَارِ ۞

9. O He Who transforms sadness to relief and joy,

10. O He Who is the Deity of all past and future beings,

All-Glorified are You; there is no deity but You!
Mercy! Mercy! Protect us from the Fire!

53

1. O the Lord of Paradise and Hell,

2. O the Lord of the Prophets and the virtuous,

3. O the Lord of the truthful and the godly,

4. O the Lord of the small and the great,

5. O the Lord of the kernels, seeds, and the fruit,

6. O Lord of the rivers and trees,

7. O the Lord of the deserts and wastelands,

يَا رَبَّ الْعَبِيدِ وَالْأَحْرَارِ ۞

يَا رَبَّ الْإِعْلَانِ وَالْإِسْرَارِ ۞

يَا رَبَّ اللَّيْلِ وَالنَّهَارِ ۞

سُبْحَانَكَ يَا لَا إِلٰهَ إِلَّا أَنْتَ الْأَمَانَ الْأَمَانَ

اَجِرْنَا مِنَ النَّارِ ۵۳

۞ يَا مَنْ لِحِوَ فِي كُلِّ شَيْءٍ عِلْمُهُ

۞ يَا مَنْ نَفَذَ بِكُلِّ شَيْءٍ بَصَرُهُ

۞ يَا مَنْ بَلَغَتْ إِلَى كُلِّ شَيْءٍ قُدْرَتُهُ

۞ يَا مَنْ لَا يُحْصِى الْعِبَادُ نَعْمَاءَهُ

۞ يَا مَنْ لَا تَبْلُغُ الْخَلَائِقُ شُكْرَهُ

۞ يَا مَنْ لَا تُدْرِكُ الْأَفْهَامُ جَلَالَهُ

8. O the Lord of the slaves and the free,

9. O the Lord of everything apparent or hidden,

10. O the Lord of the night and the day,

All-Glorified are You; there is no deity but You!
Mercy! Mercy! Protect us from the Fire!

54

1. O He Whose Knowledge comprehends everything,

2. O He Whose Vision penetrates everything, without any impediment,

3. O He Whose Power is capable of everything,

4. O He Whose gifts His servants cannot number,

5. O He Whom His creatures cannot thank sufficiently,

6. O He Whose Majesty minds cannot comprehend,

يَا مَنْ لَا تَنَالُ الْأَوْهَامُ كُنْهَهُ ۞

يَا مَنِ الْعَظَمَةُ وَالْكِبْرِيَاءُ رِدَاؤُهُ ۞

يَا مَنِ الْهَيْبَةُ وَالسُّلْطَانُ بَهَاؤُهُ ۞

يَا مَنْ تَعَزَّزَ بِالْعِزِّ بَقَاؤُهُ ۞

سُبْحَانَكَ يَا لَا إِلَهَ إِلَّا أَنْتَ الْأَمَانَ الْأَمَانَ

أَجِرْنَا مِنَ النَّارِ ۞٥٤۞

يَا مَنْ لَهُ الْمَثَلُ الْأَعْلَى ۞

يَا مَنْ لَهُ الصِّفَاتُ الْعُلَى ۞

يَا مَنْ لَهُ الْآخِرَةُ وَالْأُولَى ۞

يَا مَنْ لَهُ الْجَنَّةُ الْمَأْوَى ۞

يَا مَنْ لَهُ النَّارُ وَاللَّظَى ۞

٤٩

7. O He Whose reality and nature intellects and imaginations cannot grasp,

8. O He Whose Grandeur and Sublimity are His "garment" which veils Him,

9. O He Whose Majesty and Authority are the glory of His Essence,

10. O He Who has exaltation in the honor and mightiness of being everlasting,

All-Glorified are You; there is no deity but You!
Mercy! Mercy! Protect us from the Fire!

55

1. O He to Whom the highest example applies,

2. O He to Whom belong the most sublime attributes,

3. O He to Whom the Hereafter and this world belong,

4. O He Who is the owner of the Heavenly Garden of Refuge and Dwelling,

5. O He Who is the owner of the Fire and the Furious Flame,

يَا مَنْ لَهُ الْآيَاتُ الْكُبْرَى ۞

يَا مَنْ لَهُ الْأَسْمَاءُ الْحُسْنَى ۞

يَا مَنْ لَهُ الْحُكْمُ وَالْقَضَى ۞

يَا مَنْ لَهُ السَّمَوَاتُ الْعُلَى ۞

يَا مَنْ لَهُ الْعَرْشُ وَالثَّرَى ۞

سُبْحَانَكَ يَا لَا إِلَهَ إِلَّا أَنْتَ الْأَمَانَ الْأَمَانَ

أَجِرْنَا مِنَ النَّارِ ۞٥٥

وَأَسْأَلُكَ بِأَسْمَائِكَ يَا عَفُوُّ ۞ يَا غَفُورُ ۞

يَا وَدُودُ ۞ يَا شَكُورُ ۞ يَا صَبُورُ ۞ رَؤُوفُ ۞

يَا عَطُوفُ ۞ يَا قُدُّوسُ ۞ يَا حَيُّ ۞ يَا قَيُّومُ ۞

سُبْحَانَكَ يَا لَا إِلَهَ إِلَّا أَنْتَ الْأَمَانَ الْأَمَانَ

6. O He for Whom the most supreme evidence and signs exist,

7. O He to Whom the All-Beautiful Names belong,

8. O He to Whom rule and judgment belong,

9. O He to Whom the highest heavens belong,

10. O He to Whom the Supreme Throne and the earth belong,

All-Glorified are You; there is no deity but You!
Mercy! Mercy! Protect us from the Fire!

56

I entreat You by Your Names:

1. O the All-Pardoning (Who overlooks the faults of His servants, Who grants remission and excuses much,

2. O the All-Forgiving,

3. O the All-Loving and All-Beloved, the One Who cares with tenderness,

4. O the All-Responsive (to the gratitude of His creatures),

5. O the All-Patient (Whom no haste induces to rush into an action),

6. O the All-Affectionate,

7. O the Most-Kind, who has infinite mercy,

8. O the All-Holy and All-Pure (Who is absolutely free of any defect and keeps the universe pure),

9. O the All-Living, Who always exists,

10. O the Self-Subsisting (by Whom all subsist)

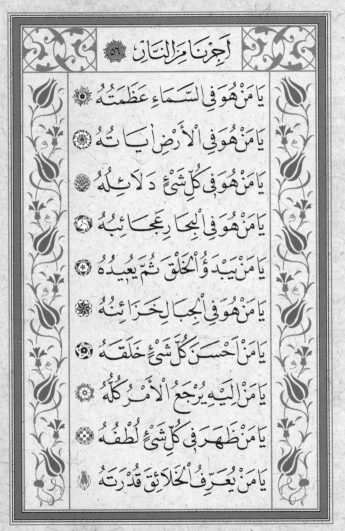

أَجِرْنَا مِنَ النَّارِ ﴿٥٦﴾

يَا مَنْ هُوَ فِي السَّمَاءِ عَظَمَتُهُ ۞

يَا مَنْ هُوَ فِي الْأَرْضِ أَيَاتُهُ ۞

يَا مَنْ هُوَ فِي كُلِّ شَيْءٍ دَلَائِلُهُ ۞

يَا مَنْ هُوَ فِي الْبِحَارِ عَجَائِبُهُ ۞

يَا مَنْ يَبْدَأُ الْخَلْقَ ثُمَّ يُعِيدُهُ ۞

يَا مَنْ هُوَ فِي الْجِبَالِ خَزَائِنُهُ ۞

يَا مَنْ أَحْسَنَ كُلَّ شَيْءٍ خَلَقَهُ ۞

يَا مَنْ إِلَيْهِ يَرْجِعُ الْأَمْرُ كُلُّهُ ۞

يَا مَنْ ظَهَرَ فِي كُلِّ شَيْءٍ لُطْفُهُ ۞

يَا مَنْ يُعَرِّفُ الْخَلَائِقَ قُدْرَتَهُ ۞

All-Glorified are You; there is no deity but You!
Mercy! Mercy! Protect us from the Fire!

57

1. O He Whose glory and might are in the heavens,

2. O He Whose signs are all over the earth,

3. O He Whose evidence is in everything,

4. O He Whose amazing creatures and acts are in the seas,

5. O He Who originates creation, then brings it forth anew,

6. O He Whose treasures are in the mountains,

7. O He Who makes whatever He creates in the best manner,

8. O He to Whom all matters are referred,

9. O He Whose kindness and bountifulness are manifest in all things,

10. O He Who makes His Power known to His creatures,

سُبْحَانَكَ يَا لَا إِلٰهَ إِلَّا أَنْتَ الْأَمَانَ الْأَمَانَ

أَجِرْنَا مِنَ النَّارِ ۝٥٧

يَا حَجِيبَ مَنْ لَا حَجِيبَ لَهُ ۞

يَا طَبِيبَ مَنْ لَا طَبِيبَ لَهُ ۞

يَا مُجِيبَ مَنْ لَا مُجِيبَ لَهُ ۞

يَا شَفِيقَ مَنْ لَا شَفِيقَ لَهُ ۞

يَا رَفِيقَ مَنْ لَا رَفِيقَ لَهُ ۞

يَا شَفِيعَ مَنْ لَا شَفِيعَ لَهُ ۞

يَا مُغِيثَ مَنْ لَا مُغِيثَ لَهُ ۞

يَا دَلِيلَ مَنْ لَا دَلِيلَ لَهُ ۞

يَا قَائِدَ مَنْ لَا قَائِدَ لَهُ ۞

۵۲

All-Glorified are You; there is no deity but You!
Mercy! Mercy! Protect us from the Fire!

58

1. O He Who is the beloved of those who have no beloved,
2. O He Who is the healer of those who have no curers,
3. O He Who answers the calls and prayers of those who have no one to answer their call,
4. O He Who has affection on those who have no one to show them affection,
5. O He Who is the friend of those who have no friends,
6. O He Who is the intercessor for those who have no interceders,
7. O He Who is the aid of those who have no one to aid them,
8. O He Who is the guide for those who have no one to guide them,
9. O He Who is the leader of those who have no one to lead them,

يَا رَاحِمَ مَنْ لَا رَاحِمَ لَهُ

سُبْحَانَكَ يَا لَا إِلٰهَ إِلَّا أَنْتَ الْأَمَانَ الْأَمَانَ

اَجِرْنَا مِنَ النَّارِ ﴿٥٨﴾

يَا كَافِى مَنِ اسْتَكْفَاهُ ۞

يَا هَادِى مَنِ اسْتَهْدَاهُ ۞

يَا كَالِى مَنِ اسْتَكْلَاهُ ۞

يَا دَاعِى مَنِ اسْتَدْعَاهُ ۞

يَا شَافِى مَنِ اسْتَشْفَاهُ ۞

يَا قَاضِى مَنِ اسْتَقْضَاهُ ۞

يَا مُغْنِى مَنِ اسْتَغْنَاهُ ۞

يَا مُوفِى مَنِ اسْتَوْفَاهُ ۞

10. O He Who has compassion on those who have no one to show them compassion,

All-Glorified are You; there is no deity but You!
Mercy! Mercy! Protect us from the Fire!

59

1. O He Who suffices for anyone who turns to Him in need,

2. O He Who guides anyone who asks Him for guidance,

3. O He Who satisfies the needs of anyone who asks Him for help,

4. O He Who responds to anyone who prays to Him to enter Paradise,

5. O He Who heals anyone who asks Him for cure,

6. O He Who fulfills the needs of anyone who seeks from Him,

7. O He Who bestows riches on anyone who asks Him for riches,

8. O He Who takes care of the affairs of those who so request,

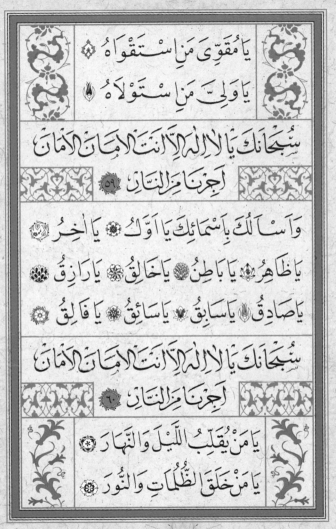

يَا مُقْوِى مَنِ اسْتَقْوَاهُ ۞

يَا وَلِىَّ مَنِ اسْتَوْلَاهُ ۞

سُبْحَانَكَ يَا لَا إِلَهَ إِلَّا أَنْتَ الْأَمَانَ الْأَمَانَ

أَجِرْنَا مِنَ النَّارِ ۵۹

وَأَسْأَلُكَ بِأَسْمَائِكَ يَا أَوَّلُ ۞ يَا آخِرُ ۞

يَا ظَاهِرُ ۞ يَا بَاطِنُ ۞ يَا خَالِقُ ۞ يَا رَازِقُ ۞

يَا صَادِقُ ۞ يَا سَابِقُ ۞ يَا سَائِقُ ۞ يَا فَالِقُ ۞

سُبْحَانَكَ يَا لَا إِلَهَ إِلَّا أَنْتَ الْأَمَانَ الْأَمَانَ

أَجِرْنَا مِنَ النَّارِ ۶۰

يَا مَنْ يُقَلِّبُ اللَّيْلَ وَالنَّهَارَ ۞

يَا مَنْ خَلَقَ الظُّلُمَاتِ وَالنُّورَ ۞

۵٤

9.   O He Who reinforces anyone who asks Him for power,
10. O He Who befriends and protects anyone who asks Him for friendship or protection,

All-Glorified are You; there is no deity but You!

Mercy! Mercy! Protect us from the Fire!

60

I entreat You by Your Names:

1.   O the First, (before Whom nothing existed,)
2.   O the Last One, (Whom nothing survives or outlives),
3.   O the All-Outward, (above Whom there is nothing and to Whom the lives and formations of all things point),
4.   O the All-Inward, (underneath Whom there is nothing, to Whom nuclei or seeds point, Who is concealed from the vision of creatures, Whom no eye can see, nor any comprehension conceive,)
5.   O the Creator,
6.   O the All-Providing (Who is the guarantor of provisions),
7.   O the All-Truthful,
8.   O the All-Preceding,
9.   O the All-Impelling, (Who impels each being toward the purpose of its creation and toward attainable perfection,
10. O the All-Splitting, (Who splits grains and kernels and makes them sprout and Who brings out the day from the night and the night from the day,)

All-Glorified are You; there is no deity but You!

Mercy! Mercy! Protect us from the Fire!

61

1.   O He Who alternates night and day,
2.   O He Who creates veils of darkness and light,

يَا مَنْ جَعَلَ الظِّلَّ وَالْحَرُورَ ۞

يَا مَنْ سَخَّرَ الشَّمْسَ وَالْقَمَرَ ۞

يَا مَنْ خَلَقَ الْمَوْتَ وَالْحَيوةَ ۞

يَا مَنْ لَهُ الْخَلْقُ وَالْأَمْرُ ۞

يَا مَنْ لَمْ يَتَّخِذْ صَاحِبَةً وَلَا وَلَدًا ۞

يَا مَنْ لَمْ يَكُنْ لَهُ شَرِيكٌ فِي الْمُلْكِ ۞

يَا مَنْ لَمْ يَكُنْ لَهُ وَلِيٌّ مِنَ الذُّلِّ ۞

يَا مَنْ لَهُ الْحَوْلُ وَالْقُوَّةُ ۞

سُبْحَانَكَ يَا لَا إِلٰهَ إِلَّا أَنْتَ الْأَمَانَ الْأَمَانَ نَجِّنَا مِنَ النَّارِ ۞٦١۞

يَا مَنْ يَعْلَمُ مُرَادَ الْمُرِيدِينَ

3. O He Who generates shade and heat,
4. O He Who has subjugated the sun and the moon and put them at the service of His creatures,
5. O He Who creates death and life,
6. O He to Whom the authority of creating and commanding belong,
7. O He Who is exempt from having a spouse or a child,
8. O He Who never has a partner in His Sovereignty,
9. O He Who is free from the abasement of adopting a helper,
10. O He Who is the sole and the true possessor of strength and power,

All-Glorified are You; there is no deity but You!
Mercy! Mercy! Deliver us from the Fire!

62

1. O He Who knows the requests of those who request,

يَا مَنْ يَمْلِكُ حَوَائِجَ السَّائِلِينَ ۞

يَا مَنْ يَسْمَعُ أَنِينَ الْوَالِهِينَ ۞

يَا مَنْ يَرَى بُكَاءَ الْخَائِفِينَ ۞

يَا مَنْ يَعْلَمُ ضَمِيرَ الصَّامِتِينَ ۞

يَا مَنْ يَرَى نَدَمَ النَّادِمِينَ ۞

يَا مَنْ يَقْبَلُ عُذْرَ التَّائِبِينَ ۞

يَا مَنْ لَا يُصْلِحُ عَمَلَ الْمُفْسِدِينَ ۞

يَا مَنْ لَا يُضِيعُ أَجْرَ الْمُحْسِنِينَ ۞

يَا مَنْ لَا يَبْعُدُ عَنْ قُلُوبِ الْعَارِفِينَ ۞

سُبْحَانَكَ يَا لَا إِلَهَ إِلَّا أَنْتَ الْأَمَانَ الْأَمَانَ

نَجِّنَا مِنَ النَّارِ ۞ ٦٢

٥٦

2. O He Who has wealth and power to provide the needs of those who make requests,

3. O He Who hears the laments of those who are overtaken by grief,

4. O He Who sees and is mindful of those who shed tears in dread of His punishment,

5. O He Who knows what lies in the hearts of those who keep silent,

6. O He Who sees and knows the regret of those who repent of their sins,

7. O He Who accepts the excuses of the repentant,

8. O He Who does not improve the affairs of the seditious and malevolent,

9. O He Who does not let the reward of those who do good deeds be wasted,

10. O He Who is never distant from the hearts of those who have knowledge of Him,

All-Glorified are You; there is no deity but You!
Mercy! Mercy! Deliver us from the Fire!

يَا غَافِرَ الْخَطَاءِ ۞ يَا دَائِمَ الْبَقَاءِ ۞

يَا وَاسِعَ الْعَطَاءِ ۞ يَا سَامِعَ الدُّعَاءِ ۞

يَا كَاشِفَ الْبَلَاءِ ۞ يَا رَافِعَ السَّمَاءِ ۞

يَا قَدِيمَ السَّنَاءِ ۞ يَا عَظِيمَ الثَّنَاءِ ۞

يَا شَرِيفَ الْجَزَاءِ ۞ يَا كَثِيرَ الْوَفَاءِ ۞

سُبْحَانَكَ يَا لَا اِلَهَ اِلَّا اَنْتَ الْاَمَانَ الْاَمَانَ

نَجِّنَا مِنَ النَّارِ ۲۳

وَاَسْأَلُكَ بِاَسْمَائِكَ يَا غَفَّارُ ۞ يَا سَتَّارُ ۞

يَا قَهَّارُ ۞ يَا جَبَّارُ ۞ يَا صَبَّارُ ۞ يَا رَزَّاقُ ۞

يَا فَتَّاحُ ۞ يَا عَلَّامُ ۞ يَا وَهَّابُ ۞ يَا تَوَّابُ ۞

سُبْحَانَكَ يَا لَا اِلَهَ اِلَّا اَنْتَ الْاَمَانَ الْاَمَانَ

٥٧

1. O He Who exists permanently,
2. O the Forgiver of faults,
3. O the Hearer of prayers,
4. O He Whose gifts and favors are abundant,
5. O the Raiser of the heavens,
6. O the Remover of calamities,
7. O the One of supreme praise and laudation,
8. O the One of pre-eternal splendor and loftiness,
9. O the One of profound fidelity,
10. O He Who gives the noblest reward in return,

All-Glorified are You; there is no deity but You!
Mercy! Mercy! Deliver us from the Fire!

64

I entreat You by Your Names:

1. O the All-Forgiving,
2. O the All-Veiler, (Who veils the shame, ugliness, mistakes, faults, and sins of His servants,)
3. O the All-Overwhelming, (Who dominates His servants by rule and power and Who rules them in the way He wills),
4. O the All-Compelling, (Who makes everything bow down and Who makes whatever He wills happen by force,)
5. O the All-Patient, (Who does not hasten to punish His servants who persist in rebellion and Who grants patience to His servants,)
6. O the All-Providing, (Who provides for all beings,)
7. O the One Who judges between people with truth and separates them,
8. O the All-Knowing,
9. O the All-Bestower, (Who bestows gifts and rewards on His servants in abundance, although they have no claim,)
10. O the All-Relenting One Who accepts repentance and returns it with liberal forgiveness and additional reward,

يَا مَنْ خَلَقَنِي وَسَوَّانِي ۞

يَا مَنْ رَزَقَنِي وَرَبَّانِي ۞

يَا مَنْ أَطْعَمَنِي وَسَقَانِي ۞

يَا مَنْ قَرَّبَنِي وَأَدْنَانِي ۞

يَا مَنْ عَصَمَنِي وَكَفَانِي ۞

يَا مَنْ حَفِظَنِي وَكَلَانِي ۞

يَا مَنْ وَفَّقَنِي وَهَدَانِي ۞

يَا مَنْ أَعَزَّنِي وَأَغْنَانِي ۞

يَا مَنْ أَمَاتَنِي وَأَحْيَانِي ۞

يَا مَنْ أَنَسَنِي وَآوَانِي ۞

All-Glorified are You; there is no deity but You!
Mercy! Mercy! Deliver us from the Fire!

65

1. O He Who has created me and given me the best form and nature,

2. O He Who provides for me and trains, raises, and provides for me,

3. O He Who provides me with food and drink,

4. O He Who draws me and brings me nearer to Himself,

5. O He Who safeguards me and is sufficient for me,

6. O He Who preserves me and takes care of my needs,

7. O He Who leads me to success and to the right way,

8. O He Who gives me dignity and who makes me rich,

9. O He Who will make me die and Who will resurrect me,

10. O He Who befriends and accompanies me and Who embraces me with mercy,

سُبْحَانَكَ يَا إِلَهَ إِلَّا أَنْتَ الْأَمَانَ الْأَمَانَ

نَجِّنَا مِنَ النَّارِ ﴿٦٥﴾

يَا مَنْ يُحِقُّ الْحَقَّ بِكَلِمَاتِهِ ۝

يَا مَنْ لَا مُعَقِّبَ لِحُكْمِهِ ۝

يَا مَنْ لَا رَادَّ لِقَضَائِهِ ۝

يَا مَنْ يَحُولُ بَيْنَ الْمَرْءِ وَقَلْبِهِ ۝

يَا مَنْ يَقْبَلُ التَّوْبَةَ عَنْ عِبَادِهِ ۝

يَا مَنْ لَا تَنْفَعُ الشَّفَاعَةُ إِلَّا بِإِذْنِهِ ۝

يَا مَنِ السَّمَوَاتُ مَطْوِيَّاتٌ بِيَمِينِهِ ۝

يَا مَنْ هُوَ أَعْلَمُ بِمَنْ ضَلَّ عَنْ سَبِيلِهِ ۝

يَا مَنْ يُسَبِّحُ الرَّعْدُ بِحَمْدِهِ وَالْمَلَائِكَةُ مِنْ خِيفَتِهِ ۝

All-Glorified are You; there is no deity but You!
Mercy! Mercy! Deliver us from the Fire!

<h2 style="text-align:center">66</h2>

1. O He who establishes the truth by His words,

2. O He Whose decree cannot be overruled by anybody,

3. O He Whose judgment cannot be averted by anybody,

4. O He Who enters in between people and their hearts, (Who manipulates hearts as He wills),

5. O He Who accepts repentance from His servants,

6. O He without Whose permission no intercession can be of benefit,

7. O He in Whose "right hand" the heavens are to be rolled up,

8. O He Who knows best those who deviate from His path,

9. O He Whom thunder glorifies with praise as do the angels, in awe of Him,

يَا مَنْ يُرْسِلُ الرِّيَاحَ بُشْرًا بَيْنَ يَدَىْ رَحْمَتِهِ ۞

سُبْحَانَكَ يَا لَا إِلَهَ إِلَّا أَنْتَ الْأَمَانَ الْأَمَانَ

نَجِّنَا مِنَ النَّارِ ۞٦٦

يَا مَنْ جَعَلَ الْأَرْضَ مِهَادًا ۞

يَا مَنْ جَعَلَ الْجِبَالَ أَوْتَادًا ۞

يَا مَنْ جَعَلَ الشَّمْسَ سِرَاجًا ۞

يَا مَنْ جَعَلَ الْقَمَرَ نُورًا ۞

يَا مَنْ جَعَلَ اللَّيْلَ لِبَاسًا ۞

يَا مَنْ جَعَلَ النَّهَارَ مَعَاشًا ۞

يَا مَنْ جَعَلَ النَّوْمَ سُبَاتًا ۞

يَا مَنْ جَعَلَ السَّمَاءَ بِنَاءً ۞

10. O He Who sends forth the merciful winds as glad tidings in advance of His mercy (rain),

All-Glorified are You; there is no deity but You!
Mercy! Mercy! Deliver us from the Fire!

67

1. O He Who has made the earth a cradle (for His creatures),

2. O He Who has rendered the mountains masts (for the ship of the earth),

3. O He Who has made the sun a lamp (for the palace of the earth,)

4. O He Who has made the moon a luminous candle (in the ceiling of the earth),

5. O He Who has made the night a cover,

6. O He Who has made the day a time of work and earning,

7. O He Who has made sleep a means of rest,

8. O He Who has constructed the heavens as an edifice,

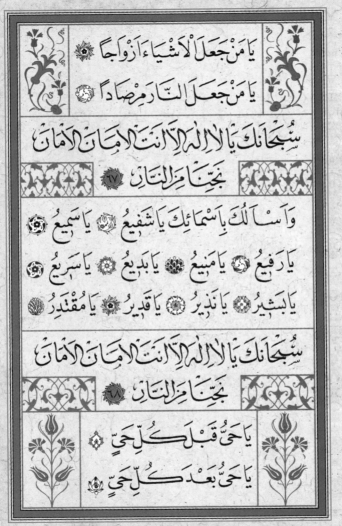

يَا مَنْ جَعَلَ الْأَشْيَاءَ أَزْوَاجًا ۝

يَا مَنْ جَعَلَ النَّارَ مِرْصَادًا ۝

سُبْحَانَكَ يَا لَا إِلَهَ إِلَّا أَنْتَ الْأَمَانَ الْأَمَانَ

نَجِّنَا مِنَ النَّارِ ۝٦٧

وَأَسْأَلُكَ بِأَسْمَائِكَ يَا شَفِيعُ ۝ يَا سَمِيعُ ۝

يَا رَفِيعُ ۝ يَا مَنِيعُ ۝ يَا بَدِيعُ ۝ يَا سَرِيعُ ۝

يَا بَشِيرُ ۝ يَا نَذِيرُ ۝ يَا قَدِيرُ ۝ يَا مُقْتَدِرُ ۝

سُبْحَانَكَ يَا لَا إِلَهَ إِلَّا أَنْتَ الْأَمَانَ الْأَمَانَ

نَجِّنَا مِنَ النَّارِ ۝٦٨

يَا حَيُّ قَبْلَ كُلِّ حَيٍّ ۝

يَا حَيُّ بَعْدَ كُلِّ حَيٍّ ۝

9. O He Who has created things in pairs,
10. O He Who has made the Fire watch over those who will
    enter it,

All-Glorified are You; there is no deity but You!
Mercy! Mercy! Deliver us from the Fire!

68

I entreat You by Your Names:

1. O the All-Interceding,
2. O the All-Hearing One,
3. O the All-Exalting,
4. O the All-Preventing,
5. O the All-Originating, Who creates in the best shape, artfully
    and without anything preceding Him to imitate,
6. O the All-Swift,
7. O the Giver of glad tidings,
8. O the All-Warning,
9. O the All-Powerful,
10. O the All-Omnipotent,

All-Glorified are You; there is no deity but You!
Mercy! Mercy! Deliver us from the Fire!

69

1. O the All-Living, Who existed before all living beings,
2. O the All-Living One, Who will exist after all living beings
    have ceased to exist,

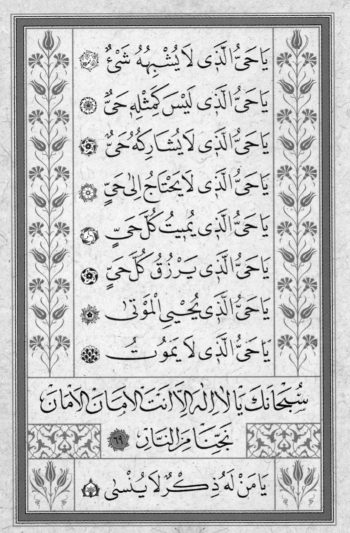

يَا حَيُّ الَّذِى لَا يُشْبِهُهُ شَىْءٌ ۞

يَا حَيُّ الَّذِى لَيْسَ كَمِثْلِهِ حَىٌّ ۞

يَا حَيُّ الَّذِى لَا يُشَارِكُهُ حَىٌّ ۞

يَا حَيُّ الَّذِى لَا يَحْتَاجُ اِلَى حَىٍّ ۞

يَا حَيُّ الَّذِى يُمِيتُ كُلَّ حَىٍّ ۞

يَا حَيُّ الَّذِى يَرْزُقُ كُلَّ حَىٍّ ۞

يَا حَيُّ الَّذِى يُحْيِى الْمَوْتَى ۞

يَا حَيُّ الَّذِى لَا يَمُوتُ ۞

سُبْحَانَكَ يَا لَا اِلٰهَ اِلَّا اَنْتَ الْاَمَانَ الْاَمَانَ
نَجِّنَا مِنَ النَّارِ ۶۹

يَا مَنْ لَهُ ذِكْرٌ لَا يُنْسَى ۞

3. O the All-Living, Whom nothing resembles,

4. O the All-Living, to Whom nothing is equal or similar,

5. O the All-Living, of whom no being can be a partner,

6. O the All-Living, Who is not in need of any living being,

7. O the All-Living, Who makes all living beings die,

8. O the All-Living, Who provides for all living beings,

9. O the All-Living, Who resurrects the dead,

10. O the All-Living, Who never dies,

All-Glorified are You; there is no deity but You!
Mercy! Mercy! Deliver us from the Fire!

70

1. O He Who is remembered without ever being forgotten,

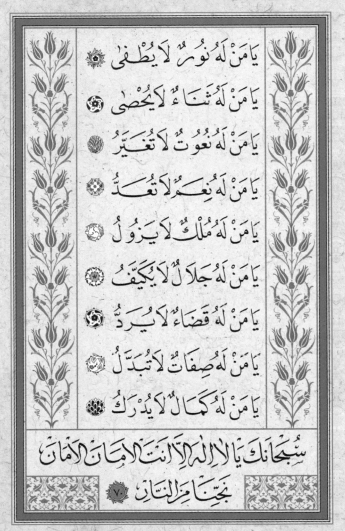

يَا مَنْ لَهُ نُورٌ لَا يُطْفَى ۞

يَا مَنْ لَهُ ثَنَاءٌ لَا يُحْصَى ۞

يَا مَنْ لَهُ نُعُوتٌ لَا تَغَيَّرُ ۞

يَا مَنْ لَهُ نِعَمٌ لَا تُعَدُّ ۞

يَا مَنْ لَهُ مُلْكٌ لَا يَزُولُ ۞

يَا مَنْ لَهُ جَلَالٌ لَا يُكَيَّفُ ۞

يَا مَنْ لَهُ قَضَاءٌ لَا يُرَدُّ ۞

يَا مَنْ لَهُ صِفَاتٌ لَا تُبَدَّلُ ۞

يَا مَنْ لَهُ كَمَالٌ لَا يُدْرَكُ ۞

سُبْحَانَكَ يَا لَا إِلَهَ إِلَّا أَنْتَ الْأَمَانَ الْأَمَانَ
نَجِّنَا مِنَ النَّارِ ۞٧

2. O He Who has a Light which is never extinguished,

3. O He Who has laudation and praise incomputable,

4. O He Who has qualities of laudation which cannot be altered,

5. O He Who has blessings uncountable,

6. O He Who has sovereignty that never decays,

7. O He Who has majesty indescribable,

8. O He Who has decree and judgment that can never be resisted or averted,

9. O He Who has attributes that cannot be changed,

10. O He Who has perfection incomprehensible,

All-Glorified are You; there is no deity but You!
Mercy! Mercy! Deliver us from the Fire!

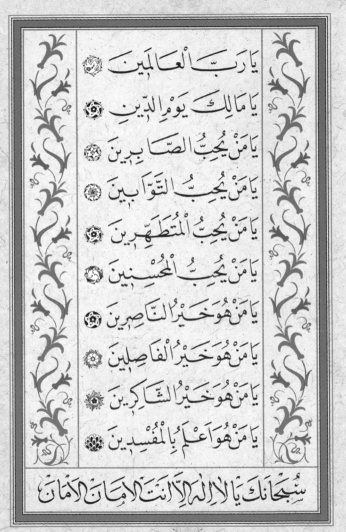

يَا رَبَّ الْعَالَمِينَ ۞

يَا مَالِكَ يَوْمِ الدِّينِ ۞

يَا مَنْ يُحِبُّ الصَّابِرِينَ ۞

يَا مَنْ يُحِبُّ التَّوَّابِينَ ۞

يَا مَنْ يُحِبُّ الْمُتَطَهِّرِينَ ۞

يَا مَنْ يُحِبُّ الْمُحْسِنِينَ ۞

يَا مَنْ هُوَ خَيْرُ النَّاصِرِينَ ۞

يَا مَنْ هُوَ خَيْرُ الْفَاصِلِينَ ۞

يَا مَنْ هُوَ خَيْرُ الشَّاكِرِينَ ۞

يَا مَنْ هُوَ أَعْلَمُ بِالْمُفْسِدِينَ ۞

سُبْحَانَكَ يَا لَا إِلَهَ إِلَّا أَنْتَ الْأَمَانَ الْأَمَانَ

1. O the Lord of the worlds,

2. O the Master of the Day of Judgment,

3. O He Who loves the patient,

4. O He Who loves the repentant,

5. O He Who loves those who purify themselves physically and spiritually,

6. O He Who loves those who worship Him as if they see Him and those who are devoted to doing good,

7. O He Who is the Best of helpers,

8. O He Who is the Best of those who judge justly and distinguish right from wrong and truth from falsehood,

9. O He Who is the Best of those who respond to the gratitude shown,

10. O He Who best knows the seditious and malevolent,

All-Glorified are You; there is no deity but You!
Mercy! Mercy! Deliver us from the Fire!

نَجِّنَا مِنَ النَّارِ ﴿٧١﴾

وَأَسْأَلُكَ بِأَسْمَائِكَ يَا مُبْدِئُ ۞ يَا مُعِيدُ ۞

يَا حَفِيظُ ۞ يَا مُحِيطُ ۞ يَا حَمِيدُ ۞ يَا مَجِيدُ ۞

يَا مُقِيتُ ۞ يَا مُغِيثُ ۞ يَا مُعِزُّ ۞ يَا مُذِلُّ ۞

سُبْحَانَكَ يَا لَا إِلٰهَ إِلَّا أَنْتَ الْأَمَانَ الْأَمَانَ

نَجِّنَا مِنَ النَّارِ ﴿٧٢﴾

يَا مَنْ هُوَ أَحَدٌ بِلَا ضِدٍّ ۞

يَا مَنْ هُوَ فَرْدٌ بِلَا نِدٍّ ۞

يَا مَنْ هُوَ صَمَدٌ بِلَا عَيْبٍ ۞

يَا مَنْ هُوَ وِتْرٌ بِلَا شَفْعٍ ۞

يَا مَنْ هُوَ رَبٌّ بِلَا وَزِيرٍ ۞

٦٥

72

I entreat You by Your Names:

1. O the All-Commencing, (Who creates beings out of nothing and without a pre-existing model,

2. O the All-Reproducing, Who brings creation anew,

3. O the All-Preserving,

4. O the All-Comprehensive, (Who comprehends everything in His Names and Attributes and from Whom nothing can be hidden,)

5. O the All-Praiseworthy, (for Whom is all praise, whoever gives it to whomever for whatever reason and in whatever way, from the first day of creation until eternity,)

6. O the All-Sublime, (Who has utmost honor and might and Whose kindness and beneficence are all-extensive,)

7. O the All-Sustaining,

8. O the All-Succoring,

9. O the All-Exalting and Honoring,

10. O the All-Abasing,

All-Glorified are You; there is no deity but You!
Mercy! Mercy! Deliver us from the Fire!

73

1. O the Unique One of absolute Unity, Who has no opposites,

2. O the All-Independent, Single One,

3. O the Eternally Besought-of-All, Who is free from all shame and defects,

4. O the All-Unique, to Whom nothing can ever be similar,

5. O He Who is in need of no assistance nor aids,

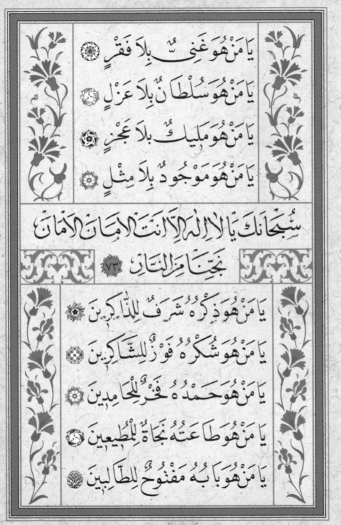

يَا مَنْ هُوَ غَنِيٌّ بِلَا فَقْرٍ ۞

يَا مَنْ هُوَ سُلْطَانٌ بِلَا عَزْلٍ ۞

يَا مَنْ هُوَ مَلِيكٌ بِلَا عَجْزٍ ۞

يَا مَنْ هُوَ مَوْجُودٌ بِلَا مِثْلٍ ۞

سُبْحَانَكَ يَا لَا إِلٰهَ إِلَّا أَنْتَ الْأَمَانَ الْأَمَانَ

نَجِّنَا مِنَ النَّارِ ۷۳

يَا مَنْ هُوَ ذِكْرُهُ شَرَفٌ لِلذَّاكِرِينَ ۞

يَا مَنْ هُوَ شُكْرُهُ فَوْزٌ لِلشَّاكِرِينَ ۞

يَا مَنْ هُوَ حَمْدُهُ فَخْرٌ لِلْحَامِدِينَ ۞

يَا مَنْ هُوَ طَاعَتُهُ نَجَاةٌ لِلْمُطِيعِينَ ۞

يَا مَنْ هُوَ بَابُهُ مَفْتُوحٌ لِلطَّالِبِينَ ۞

6. O the All-Wealthy, Who is exempt from poverty,

7. O the absolute, eternal Authority, Who cannot be deposed,

8. O the All-Sovereign, Who is free from impotence,

9. O the All-Existent, Who has no equals or peers,

All-Glorified are You; there is no deity but You!
Mercy! Mercy! Deliver us from the Fire!

74

1. O He Whose remembrance is an honor for those who remember Him,

2. O He for Whom thanksgiving is a triumph for the thankful,

3. O He for Whom praise is a pride for those who praise Him,

4. O He to Whom obedience is salvation for those who obey Him,

5. O He Whose door is open to those who seek Him,

يَا مَنْ هُوَ سَبِيلُهُ وَاضِحٌ لِلْمُؤْمِنِينَ ۞

يَا مَنْ هُوَ آيَاتُهُ بُرْهَانٌ لِلنَّاظِرِينَ ۞

يَا مَنْ هُوَ كِتَابُهُ تَذْكِرَةٌ لِلْمُوقِنِينَ ۞

يَا مَنْ هُوَ عَفْوُهُ مَلْجَأٌ لِلْمُذْنِبِينَ ۞

يَا مَنْ هُوَ رَحْمَتُهُ قَرِيبٌ لِلْمُحْسِنِينَ ۞

سُبْحَانَكَ يَا لَا إِلَهَ إِلَّا أَنْتَ الْأَمَانَ الْأَمَانَ

نَجِّنَا مِنَ النَّارِ ۷٤

يَا مَنْ تَبَارَكَ اسْمُهُ ۞ يَا مَنْ تَعَالَى جَدُّهُ ۞

يَا مَنْ جَلَّ ثَنَاؤُهُ ۞ يَا مَنْ لَا إِلَهَ غَيْرُهُ ۞

يَا مَنْ تَقَدَّسَتْ أَسْمَاؤُهُ ۞ يَا مَنْ يَدُومُ بَقَاؤُهُ ۞

يَا مَنِ الْعَظَمَةُ بَهَاؤُهُ ۞ يَا مَنِ الْكِبْرِيَاءُ رِدَاؤُهُ ۞

٦٧

6. O He Whose path is evident and clear to those who believe in Him,

7. O He Whose signs are evidence and proof for those who look and see,

8. O He Whose Book is advice and an instruction for those who have certainty of belief,

9. O He Whose pardoning is a shelter for sinners,

10. O He Whose mercy is near to those who are devoted to doing good, aware that God sees them,

All-Glorified are You; there is no deity but You!
Mercy! Mercy! Deliver us from the Fire!

75

1. O He Whose Name is exalted and holy,

2. O He Whose glory and status are transcending,

3. O He Whose laudation and praise are sublime,

4. O He save Whom there is no deity,

5. O He Whose Names are sacred and free from any imperfection,

6. O He Whose existence is unending,

7. O He Whose Grandeur is His "adornment,"

8. O He Whose Sublimity is His "garment" which veils Him,

يَا مَنْ لَا يُحْصِى الْآؤُهُ ۞ يَا مَنْ لَا يُعَدُّ نَعْمَاؤُهُ ۞

سُبْحَانَكَ يَا لَا إِلَهَ إِلَّا أَنْتَ الْأَمَانَ الْأَمَانَ

نَجِّنَا مِنَ النَّارِ ۷۵

وَأَسْأَلُكَ بِأَسْمَائِكَ يَا مُعِينُ ۞ يَا مُبِينُ ۞

يَا أَمِينُ ۞ يَا مَكِينُ ۞ يَا مَتِينُ ۞ يَا شَدِيدُ ۞

يَا شَهِيدُ ۞ يَا رَشِيدُ ۞ يَا حَمِيدُ ۞ يَا مَجِيدُ ۞

سُبْحَانَكَ يَا لَا إِلَهَ إِلَّا أَنْتَ الْأَمَانَ الْأَمَانَ

نَجِّنَا مِنَ النَّارِ ۷۶

يَا ذَا الْعَرْشِ الْمَجِيدِ ۞ يَا ذَا الْقَوْلِ السَّدِيدِ ۞

يَا ذَا الْفَضْلِ الرَّشِيدِ ۞ يَا ذَا الْبَطْشِ الشَّدِيدِ ۞

يَا ذَا الْوَعْدِ وَالْوَعِيدِ ۞ يَا قَرِيبًا غَيْرَ بَعِيدٍ ۞

9.   O He Whose favors are incomputable,
10. O He Whose bounties are uncountable,

All-Glorified are You; there is no deity but You!
Mercy! Mercy! Deliver us from the Fire!

76

I entreat You by Your Names:
1.   O the All-Aiding,
2.   O the All-Evident, (from Whom nothing is hidden and Who makes all truth manifest,)
3.   O the All-Trustworthy, (Who is faithful to His promise and word and Who gives security and peace to His creatures,)
4.   O He Who is firmly established in power and Whose sovereignty is unshakeable,
5.   O the All-Firm, (Whose power and strength are absolute,)
6.   O the All-Severe, (Whose punishment is severe,)
7.   O the All-Witnessing, from Whom nothing can be hidden and Who never forgets,
8.   O the All-Right, Guiding One,
9.   O the All-Praiseworthy, (for Whom is all praise, whoever gives it to whomever for whatever reason and in whatever way, from the first day of creation until eternity,)
10. O the All-Sublime, (Who has utmost honor and might and Whose kindness and beneficence are all-extensive,)

All-Glorified are You; there is no deity but You!
Mercy! Mercy! Deliver us from the Fire!

77

1.   O He Who is the Possessor of the Sublime, Supreme Throne,
2.   O He Who is the Possessor of the most truthful word,
3.   O He Who is the Possessor of the most proper grace and bounty,
4.   O He Who is the Possessor of the severe grip,
5.   O He Who is the Owner of both promise and threat,
6.   O He Who is the All-Near, without ever being distant,

يَا مَنْ هُوَ الْوَلِيُّ الْحَمِيدُ ۞

يَا مَنْ هُوَ عَلَى كُلِّ شَيْءٍ شَهِيدٌ ۞

يَا مَنْ هُوَ لَيْسَ بِظَلَّامٍ لِلْعَبِيدِ ۞

يَا مَنْ هُوَ أَقْرَبُ إِلَيْهِ مِنْ حَبْلِ الْوَرِيدِ ۞

سُبْحَانَكَ يَا لَا إِلَهَ إِلَّا أَنْتَ الْأَمَانَ الْأَمَانَ نَجِّنَا مِنَ النَّارِ ۞٧٧

يَا مَنْ لَا شَرِيكَ لَهُ وَلَا وَزِيرَ ۞

يَا مَنْ لَا شَبِيهَ لَهُ وَلَا نَظِيرَ ۞

يَا خَالِقَ الشَّمْسِ وَالْقَمَرِ الْمُنِيرِ ۞

يَا مُغْنِيَ الْبَائِسِ الْفَقِيرِ ۞

يَا رَازِقَ الطِّفْلِ الصَّغِيرِ ۞

7. O He Who is the All-Guardian and the All-Praiseworthy,

8. O He Who is the All-Witnessing over all things,

9. O He Who never wrongs His servants,

10. O He Who is nearer to His servants than their own jugular vein,

All-Glorified are You; there is no deity but You!
Mercy! Mercy! Deliver us from the Fire!

78

1. O He Who has neither a partner nor an aid,

2. O He Who has neither a peer nor an equal,

3. O He Who is the Creator of both the sun and the luminous moon,

4. O He Who enriches the poor in misery,

5. O He Who provides for infants,

يَا رَاحِمَ الشَّيْخِ الْكَبِيرِ ۞

يَا عِصْمَةَ الْخَائِفِ الْمُسْتَجِيرِ ۞

يَا مَنْ هُوَ بِعِبَادِهِ بَصِيرٌ ۞

يَا مَنْ هُوَ بِجَوَائِجِ الْعِبَادِ خَبِيرٌ ۞

يَا مَنْ هُوَ عَلَى كُلِّ شَيْءٍ قَدِيرٌ ۞

سُبْحَانَكَ يَا لَا إِلَهَ إِلَّا أَنْتَ الْأَمَانَ الْأَمَانَ نَجِّنَا مِنَ النَّارِ ۷۸

يَا ذَا الْجُودِ وَالنِّعَمِ ۞ يَا ذَا الْفَضْلِ وَالْكَرَمِ ۞

يَا ذَا الْبَأْسِ وَالنِّقَمِ ۞ يَا خَالِقَ اللَّوْحِ وَالْقَلَمِ ۞

يَا بَارِئَ الذَّرِّ وَالنَّسَمِ ۞ يَا مُلْهِمَ الْعَرَبِ وَالْعَجَمِ ۞

يَا كَاشِفَ الضُّرِّ وَالْأَلَمِ ۞ يَا عَالِمَ السِّرِّ وَالْهَمَمِ ۞

6. O He Who has mercy on the helpless elderly,

7. O He Who is the reliable refuge of those who fear and seek His protection,

8. O He Who sees His servants perfectly,

9. O He Who is absolutely aware of the needs of His servants,

10. O He Who has full power over everything,

All-Glorified are You; there is no deity but You!
Mercy! Mercy! Deliver us from the Fire!

79

1. O He Who has generosity and bounty,

2. O He Who has limitless grace and munificence,

3. O He Who sends severe scourge and harsh punishments,

4. O the Creator of the Supreme Preserved Tablet and the Pen,

5. O the All-Holy Creator of minutest particles and seeds as well as humans and other living beings,

6. O He Who inspires in both the Arabs and other nations,

7. O the Remover of harm and suffering,

8. O the Knower of secrets and unexpressed intents,

يَا مَنْ لَهُ الْبَيْتُ وَالْحَرَمُ ۞ يَا مَنْ يَخْلُقُ الْأَشْيَاءَ مِنَ الْعَدَمِ ۞

سُبْحَانَكَ يَا لَا إِلٰهَ إِلَّا أَنْتَ الْأَمَانُ الْأَمَانُ نَجِّنَا مِنَ النَّارِ ۞٧٩

وَأَسْأَلُكَ بِأَسْمَائِكَ يَا عَادِلُ ۞ يَا قَابِلُ ۞ يَا فَاضِلُ ۞ يَا فَاعِلُ ۞ يَا كَافِلُ ۞ يَا جَاعِلُ ۞ يَا كَامِلُ ۞ يَا فَاطِرُ ۞ يَا طَالِبُ ۞ يَا مَطْلُوبُ ۞

سُبْحَانَكَ يَا لَا إِلٰهَ إِلَّا أَنْتَ الْأَمَانُ الْأَمَانُ نَجِّنَا مِنَ النَّارِ ۞٨٠

يَا مَنْ أَنْعَمَ بِجُودِهِ ۞ يَا مَنْ أَكْرَمَ بِطَوْلِهِ ۞ يَا مَنْ عَادَ بِلُطْفِهِ ۞ يَا مَنْ تَعَزَّزَ بِقُدْرَتِهِ ۞

9. O He Who owns the Sacred House Ka'ba, and its sanctuary,
10. O He Who has created all beings out of nothing,

All-Glorified are You; there is no deity but You!
Mercy! Mercy! Deliver us from the Fire!

80

I entreat You by Your Names:

1. O the All-Just,
2. O the All-Welcoming One, (Who welcomes the worship, prayer, repentance, supplication, and refuge of His servants,)
3. O the All-Gracious, Who gives freely,
4. O the All-Doing, (the true possessor and cause of all actions and deeds,)
5. O the All-Guaranteeing, (Who undertakes to provide the basic food of His creatures,)
6. O the All-Rendering and Performing, (Who is the true, ultimate performer of every deed and formation in the universe,)
7. O the All-Perfect,
8. O the All-Originating, (Who creates everything with a unique individuality,)
9. O the All-Demanding, (Who wills good for all beings and Who orders them to attain His approval,)
10. O the All-Sought, (Who is and must be sought after,)

All-Glorified are You; there is no deity but You!
Mercy! Mercy! Deliver us from the Fire!

81

1. O He Who grants with His infinite power,
2. O He Who gives abundantly of His infinite generosity and wealth,
3. O He Who bestows of His grace time after time,
4. O He Who shows His glory and might with His limitless power,

يَا مَنْ قَدَّرَ بِحِكْمَتِهِ ۞ يَا مَنْ حَكَمَ بِتَدْبِيرِهِ ۞

يَا مَنْ دَبَّرَ بِعِلْمِهِ ۞ يَا مَنْ تَجَاوَزَ بِحِلْمِهِ ۞

يَا مَنْ دَنَا فِي عُلُوِّهِ ۞ يَا مَنْ عَلَا فِي دُنُوِّهِ ۞

سُبْحَانَكَ يَا لَا اِلَهَ اِلَّا اَنْتَ الْاَمَانَ الْاَمَانَ

نَجِّنَا مِنَ النَّارِ ۞

يَا مَنْ يَخْلُقُ مَا يَشَاءُ ۞

يَا مَنْ يَفْعَلُ مَا يَشَاءُ ۞

يَا مَنْ يَهْدِى مَنْ يَشَاءُ ۞

يَا مَنْ يُضِلُّ مَنْ يَشَاءُ ۞

يَا مَنْ يَغْفِرُ لِمَنْ يَشَاءُ ۞

يَا مَنْ يُعَذِّبُ مَنْ يَشَاءُ ۞

5. O He Who destines and determines with His wisdom,

6. O He Who rules and judges with His wise regulations,

7. O He Who governs properly with His knowledge,

8. O He Who overlooks the faults of His servants out of His limitless forbearance and clemency,

9. O He Who is near in His limitless transcendence,

10. O He Who is limitlessly exalted in His nearness,

All-Glorified are You; there is no deity but You!
Mercy! Mercy! Deliver us from the Fire!

82

1. O He Who creates whatever He wills,

2. O He Who does whatever He wills,

3. O He Who guides to the Straight Path whomever He wills,

4. O He Who leads astray whomever He wills,

5. O He Who forgives whomever He wills,

6. O He Who punishes whomever He wills,

يَا مَنْ يَتُوبُ عَلَى مَنْ يَشَاءُ ۞

يَا مَنْ يُصَوِّرُ فِي الْأَرْحَامِ كَيْفَ يَشَاءُ ۞

يَا مَنْ يَزِيدُ فِي الْخَلْقِ مَا يَشَاءُ ۞

يَا مَنْ يَخْتَصُّ بِرَحْمَتِهِ مَنْ يَشَاءُ ۞

سُبْحَانَكَ يَا لَا إِلَهَ إِلَّا أَنْتَ الْأَمَانُ الْأَمَانُ
نَجِّنَا مِنَ النَّارِ ۞ ٨٣

يَا مَنْ لَمْ يَتَّخِذْ صَاحِبَةً وَلَا وَلَدًا ۞

يَا مَنْ لَا يُشْرِكُ فِي حُكْمِهِ أَحَدًا ۞

يَا مَنْ جَعَلَ لِكُلِّ شَيْءٍ قَدْرًا ۞

يَا مَنْ لَمْ يَزَلْ رَحِيمًا ۞

يَا جَاعِلَ الْمَلَائِكَةِ رُسُلًا ۞

7. O He Who leads whomever He wills to repentance and accepts repentance from whomever He wills,

8. O He Who forms the fetuses in wombs however He wills,

9. O He Who enhances the capabilities and gifts He bestows to His servants to whatever degree He wills,

10. O He Who allots His mercy to whomever He wills,

All-Glorified are You; there is no deity but You!
Mercy! Mercy! Deliver us from the Fire!

83

1. O He Who has never taken either a spouse or a child,

2. O He Who has never taken a partner in His rule or judgment,

3. O He Who has decreed a certain measure for everything,

4. O He Who has never ceased to be compassionate,

5. O He Who has appointed envoys from among the angels,

يَا مَنْ جَعَلَ فِي السَّمَاءِ بُرُوجًا ۞

يَا مَنْ جَعَلَ الْأَرْضَ قَرَارًا ۞

يَا مَنْ جَعَلَ مِنَ الْمَاءِ بَشَرًا ۞

يَا مَنْ أَحْصَى كُلَّ شَيْءٍ عَدَدًا ۞

يَا مَنْ أَحَاطَ بِكُلِّ شَيْءٍ عِلْمًا ۞

سُبْحَانَكَ يَا لَا إِلَهَ إِلَّا أَنْتَ الْأَمَانَ الْأَمَانَ

نَجِّنَا مِنَ النَّارِ ۞ ٨٣

وَأَسْأَلُكَ بِأَسْمَائِكَ يَا فَرْدُ ۞ يَا وِتْرُ ۞

يَا أَحَدُ ۞ يَا صَمَدُ ۞ يَا مَجْدُ ۞ يَا أَعَزُّ ۞

يَا أَجَلُّ ۞ يَا أَحَقُّ ۞ يَا أَبَرُّ ۞ يَا أَبَدُ ۞

سُبْحَانَكَ يَا لَا إِلَهَ إِلَّا أَنْتَ الْأَمَانَ الْأَمَانَ

٧٤

6. O He Who has brought out constellations in the heavens,

7. O He Who has given the earth stability and made it a secure dwelling,

8. O He Who has created human beings out of fluid,

9. O He Who has established everything, one by one, with exact measure,

10. O He Who comprehends everything in His knowledge,

All-Glorified are You; there is no deity but You!
Mercy! Mercy! Deliver us from the Fire!

84

I entreat You by Your Names:

1. O the All-Independent, Single One,

2. O the All-Unique, (to Whom nothing is equal with regard to His Essence, Attributes, Names, or acts,)

3. O the Unique One of absolute Unity,

4. O the Eternally Besought-of-All, Whom everything is in need of yet Who needs nothing,

5. O the All-Sublime and Glorious,

6. O the All-Glorious with irresistible might

7. O the All-Majestic,

8. O the Ultimate Truth and Ever-Constant,

9. O the All-Benign,

10. O the All-Eternal,

يَا مَعْرُوفَ مَنْ عَرَفَهُ ۞ يَا مَعْبُودَ مَنْ عَبَدَهُ ۞

يَا مَشْكُورَ مَنْ شَكَرَهُ ۞ يَا مَذْكُورَ مَنْ ذَكَرَهُ ۞

يَا مَحْمُودَ مَنْ حَمِدَهُ ۞ يَا مَوْجُودَ مَنْ طَلَبَهُ ۞

يَا مَوْصُوفَ مَنْ وَحَّدَهُ ۞ يَا مَحْبُوبَ مَنْ أَحَبَّهُ ۞

يَا مَرْغُوبَ مَنْ أَرَادَهُ ۞

يَا مَقْصُودَ مَنْ أَنَابَ إِلَيْهِ ۞

سُبْحَانَكَ يَا لَا إِلَهَ إِلَّا أَنْتَ الْأَمَانَ الْأَمَانَ

يَا مَنْ لَا مُلْكَ إِلَّا مُلْكُهُ ۞

يَا مَنْ لَا يُحْصِى الْعِبَادُ ثَنَائَهُ ۞

All-Glorified are You; there is no deity but You!
Mercy! Mercy! Deliver us from the Fire!

85

1. O the All-Recognized, Who is recognized by those who have true knowledge of Him,
2. O the All-Worshiped, Whom His servants worship,
3. O the All-Thanked, to Whom the thankful offer thanks,
4. O the All-Remembered, Whom people of remembrance remember and mention,
5. O the All-Praised, Whom people of praise praise,
6. O the All-Existent, Who is ever present everywhere to those who seek Him,
7. O the All-Qualified, Who those who believe in His Oneness know by His Attributes,
8. O the All-Beloved, Who is the beloved of those who love Him,
9. O the All-Desired, Who is desired by those who long for Him,
10. O the All-Sought, Who is devotedly sought for by those who turn to Him,

All-Glorified are You; there is no deity but You!
Mercy! Mercy! Deliver us from the Fire!

86

1. O He save Whose Sovereignty there is no true sovereignty,
2. O He Whose praise and laudation His servants are unable to fulfill,

يَا مَنْ لَا تَصِفُ الْخَلَائِقُ جَلَالَهُ ۞

يَا مَنْ لَا يُدْرِكُ الْأَبْصَارُ كَمَالَهُ ۞

يَا مَنْ لَا يَبْلُغُ الْأَفْهَامُ صِفَاتِهِ ۞

يَا مَنْ لَا يَنَالُ الْأَفْكَارُ كِبْرِيَاءَهُ ۞

يَا مَنْ لَا يُحْسِنُ الْإِنْسَانُ نُعُوتَهُ ۞

يَا مَنْ لَا يَرُدُّ الْعِبَادُ قَضَاءَهُ ۞

يَا مَنْ ظَهَرَ فِي كُلِّ شَيْءٍ آيَاتُهُ ۞

سُبْحَانَكَ يَا لَا إِلَهَ إِلَّا أَنْتَ الْأَمَانَ الْأَمَانَ
نَجِّنَا مِنَ النَّارِ ۞ ٨٦

يَا حَبِيبَ الْبَكَّائِينَ ۞ يَا سَنَدَ الْمُتَوَكِّلِينَ ۞

يَا هَادِيَ الْمُصَلِّينَ ۞ يَا وَلِيَّ الْمُؤْمِنِينَ ۞

3. O He Whose Majesty creatures are unable to describe,

4. O He Whose Perfection eyes are unable to comprehend,

5. O He Whose Attributes intellects are unable to grasp,

6. O He Whose Grandeur minds are unable to perceive,

7. O He Whose Qualities of laudation humans are unable to appreciate properly,

8. O He Whose decree His servants are unable to avert,

9. O He Whose evidences and signs are apparent in all things,

All-Glorified are You; there is no deity but You!
Mercy! Mercy! Deliver us from the Fire!

87

1. O He Who is the beloved of those who weep,

2. O He Who is the support of those who place their trust in Him,

3. O He Who grants guidance to those who are astray,

4. O He Who is the guardian of believers,

يَا أَنِيسَ الذَّاكِرِينَ ۞ يَا أَقْدَرَ الْقَادِرِينَ ۞

يَا أَبْصَرَ النَّاظِرِينَ ۞ يَا أَعْلَمَ الْعَالِمِينَ ۞

يَا مَفْزَعَ الْمَلْهُوفِينَ ۞ يَا أَنْصَرَ النَّاصِرِينَ ۞

سُبْحَانَكَ يَا لَا إِلَهَ إِلَّا أَنْتَ الْأَمَانَ الْأَمَانَ

نَجِّنَا مِنَ النَّارِ ۞

وَأَسْأَلُكَ بِأَسْمَائِكَ يَا مُكْرِمُ ۞ يَا مُعَظِّمُ ۞

يَا مُنْعِمُ ۞ يَا مُعْطِي ۞ يَا مُغْنِي ۞ يَا مُحْيِي ۞

يَا مُبْدِئُ ۞ يَا مُرْضِي ۞ يَا مُنْجِي ۞ يَا مُحْسِنُ ۞

سُبْحَانَكَ يَا لَا إِلَهَ إِلَّا أَنْتَ الْأَمَانَ الْأَمَانَ

نَجِّنَا مِنَ النَّارِ ۞

يَا كَافِي كُلِّ شَيْءٍ ۞

5.   O He Who is the companion of those who remember Him,
6.   O He Whose Power is infinitely superior to all powers,
7.   O He Whose Vision is infinitely superior to the vision of those who have vision,
8.   O He Whose Knowledge is infinitely superior to the knowledge of those who have knowledge,
9.   O He Who is the shelter of the helpless in grief,
10. O He Whose help is infinitely better than all other help,

All-Glorified are You; there is no deity but You!
Mercy! Mercy! Deliver us from the Fire!

88

I entreat You by Your Names:

1.   O the All-Granting and Honoring,
2.   O the All-Exalting,
3.   O the All-Bestowing,
4.   O the All-Conferring,
5.   O the All-Enriching,
6.   O the Giver of Life and All-Reviving,
7.   O the All-Commencing,
8.   O He Who fulfills the wishes of creatures and makes them content and pleased,
9.   O the All-Delivering, (Who protects creatures from all kinds of danger,)
10. O the All-Benevolent,

All-Glorified are You; there is no deity but You!
Mercy! Mercy! Deliver us from the Fire!

89

1.   O He Who is sufficient for all the needs of all things at all times,

يا قَائِمًا عَلَى كُلِّ شَيْءٍ ۞

يا مَنْ لَا يُشْبِهُهُ شَيْءٌ ۞

يا مَنْ لَا يَزِيدُ فِي مُلْكِهِ شَيْءٌ ۞

يا مَنْ لَا يَنْقُصُ مِنْ خَزَائِنِهِ شَيْءٌ ۞

يا مَنْ لَا يَخْفَى عَلَيْهِ شَيْءٌ ۞

يا مَنْ لَيْسَ كَمِثْلِهِ شَيْءٌ ۞

يا مَنْ بِيَدِهِ مَقَالِيدُ كُلِّ شَيْءٍ ۞

يا مَنْ وَسِعَتْ رَحْمَتُهُ كُلَّ شَيْءٍ ۞

يا مَنْ يَبْقَى وَيَفْنَى كُلُّ شَيْءٍ ۞

سُبْحَانَكَ يا لَا إِلهَ إِلَّا أَنْتَ الْأَمَانُ الْأَمَانُ
نَجِّنَا مِنَ النَّارِ ۞٦٩۞

2. O He Who unceasingly maintains everything and governs it,

3. O He Whom nothing resembles in any way,

4. O He Whose wealth cannot be increased by anyone,

5. O He Whose treasures never diminish with donation,

6. O He to Whom nothing can remain hidden,

7. O He to Whom nothing is equal or similar,

8. O He Who holds the keys to everything,

9. O He Whose Mercy embraces everything,

10. O He Who lasts forever while all things perish,

All-Glorified are You; there is no deity but You!
Mercy! Mercy! Deliver us from the Fire!

يَا مَنْ لَا يَعْلَمُ الْغَيْبَ اِلَّا هُوَ ۞

يَا مَنْ لَا يَصْرِفُ السُّوءَ اِلَّا هُوَ ۞

يَا مَنْ لَا يُدَبِّرُ الْاَمْرَ اِلَّا هُوَ ۞

يَا مَنْ لَا يَغْفِرُ الذُّنُوبَ اِلَّا هُوَ ۞

يَا مَنْ لَا يُقَلِّبُ الْقَلْبَ اِلَّا هُوَ ۞

يَا مَنْ لَا يَخْلُقُ الْخَلْقَ اِلَّا هُوَ ۞

يَا مَنْ لَا يُتِمُّ النِّعْمَةَ اِلَّا هُوَ ۞

يَا مَنْ لَا يُنَزِّلُ الْغَيْثَ اِلَّا هُوَ ۞

يَا مَنْ لَا يُحْيِى الْمَوْتَى اِلَّا هُوَ ۞

يَا مَنْ لَا يُغْنِى عَلَى التَّحْقِيقِ اِلَّا هُوَ ۞

سُبْحَانَكَ يَا لَا اِلَهَ اِلَّا اَنْتَ الْاَمَانَ الْاَمَانَ

90

1. O He Who is the only one to know the Unseen,
2. O He Who is the only one to expel evil,
3. O He Who is the only one to direct and govern affairs,
4. O He Who is the only one to forgive sins,
5. O He Who is the only one to turn hearts from one state to another,
6. O He Who is the only one to create creatures,
7. O He Who is the only one to grant favors,
8. O He Who is the only one to send down rain,
9. O He Who is the only one to resurrect the dead,
10. O He Who is the only one to truly give benefit and enrich,

All-Glorified are You; there is no deity but You!
Mercy! Mercy! Deliver us from the Fire!

وَأَسْأَلُكَ بِأَسْمَائِكَ يَا كَاشِفُ ۞ يَا فَارِجُ ۞

يَا فَاتِحُ ۞ يَا نَاصِرُ ۞ يَا ضَامِنُ ۞ يَا آمِرُ ۞

يَا نَاهِى ۞ يَا رَجَا ۞ يَا مُرْتَجَا ۞ يَا عَظِيمَ الرَّجَا ۞

سُبْحَانَكَ يَا لَا إِلَهَ إِلَّا أَنْتَ الْأَمَانَ الْأَمَانَ

خَلِّصْنا مِنَ النَّارِ ۞٩١۞

يَا مُعِينَ الضُّعَفَاءِ ۞ يَا كَنْزَ الْفُقَرَاءِ ۞

يَا صَاحِبَ الْغُرَبَاءِ ۞ يَا نَاصِرَ الْأَوْلِيَاءِ ۞

يَا قَاهِرَ الْأَعْدَاءِ ۞ يَا رَافِعَ السَّمَاءِ ۞

يَا كَاشِفَ الْبَلَاءِ ۞ يَا أَنِيسَ الْأَوْلِيَاءِ ۞

يَا حَبِيبَ الْأَتْقِيَاءِ ۞ يَا إِلَهَ الْأَغْنِيَاءِ ۞

91

I entreat You by Your Names:

1. O the All-Unveiling and Removing, Who unveils all secrets and enigmas of the universe to His servants and Who saves His servants from calamity, grief, pain, and agony,
2. O the All-Liberating, Who comforts by removing grief and trouble,
3. O the All-Conquering, Who opens wide the doors of mercy, grants conquest and success, and Who rules justly,
4. O the All-Helping and Giver of victory,
5. O the All-Undertaking, Who fulfills the needs of His creatures,
6. O the All-Commanding,
7. O the All-Prohibiting, Who prohibits whatever He wills,
8. O the Source of all hope,
9. O the All-Expected,
10. O the Supreme Source of all hope and expectations,

All-Glorified are You; there is no deity but You!
Mercy! Mercy! Save us from the Fire!

92

1. O the Helper of the weak,
2. O the unending Treasure of the poor,
3. O the Patron of the destitute,
4. O the Helper of His saintly friends,
5. O the Crusher of enemies,
6. O the Raiser of the heavens,
7. O the Remover of calamities,
8. O the intimate Companion of His saintly friends,
9. O the Beloved of the pious,
10. O the Lord of the wealthy and wealth,

سُبْحَانَكَ يَا لَا إِلٰهَ إِلَّا أَنْتَ الْأَمَانَ الْأَمَانَ

﴿٩٢﴾ خَلِّصْنَا مِنَ النَّارِ

يَا أَوَّلَ كُلِّ شَيْءٍ وَآخِرَهُ ۞

يَا إِلٰهَ كُلِّ شَيْءٍ وَصَانِعَهُ ۞

يَا رَازِقَ كُلِّ شَيْءٍ وَخَالِقَهُ ۞

يَا فَاطِرَ كُلِّ شَيْءٍ وَمَلِيكَهُ ۞

يَا قَابِضَ كُلِّ شَيْءٍ وَبَاسِطَهُ ۞

يَا مُبْدِئَ كُلِّ شَيْءٍ وَمُعِيدَهُ ۞

يَا مُسَبِّبَ كُلِّ شَيْءٍ وَمُقَدِّرَهُ ۞

يَا مُرَبِّيَ كُلِّ شَيْءٍ وَمُدَبِّرَهُ ۞

يَا مُكَوِّرَ كُلِّ شَيْءٍ وَمُحَوِّلَهُ ۞

All-Glorified are You; there is no deity but You!
Mercy! Mercy! Save us from the Fire!

93

1. O He Who is prior to everything and eternally subsequent to it,

2. O He Who is the Deity of everything and its Maker,

3. O He Who is the Provider of everything and its Creator,

4. O He Who is the Originator of everything and its Sovereign,

5. O He Who is the Constricter of everything and its Expander,

6. O He Who is the Originator of everything and its Reproducer,

7. O He Who is the Cause of everything and its Determiner with unique features,

8. O He Who is the Raiser and Trainer of everything and its Governor,

9. O He Who is the Director of everything and Who transforms it from one state to another,

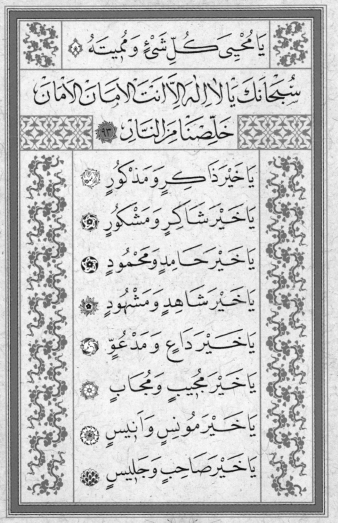

يَا مُحْيِى كُلِّ شَىْءٍ وَمُمِيتَهُ ۞

سُبْحَانَكَ يَا لَا اِلٰهَ اِلَّا اَنْتَ الْاَمَانَ الْاَمَانَ خَلِّصْنَا مِنَ النَّارِ ۞

يَا خَيْرَ ذَاكِرٍ وَمَذْكُورٍ ۞

يَا خَيْرَ شَاكِرٍ وَمَشْكُورٍ ۞

يَا خَيْرَ حَامِدٍ وَمَحْمُودٍ ۞

يَا خَيْرَ شَاهِدٍ وَمَشْهُودٍ ۞

يَا خَيْرَ دَاعٍ وَمَدْعُوٍّ ۞

يَا خَيْرَ مُجِيبٍ وَمُجَابٍ ۞

يَا خَيْرَ مُؤْنِسٍ وَاَنِيسٍ ۞

يَا خَيْرَ صَاحِبٍ وَجَلِيسٍ ۞

10. O He Who gives life to everything and makes everything die,

All-Glorified are You; there is no deity but You!
Mercy! Mercy! Save us from the Fire!

94

1. O He Who is the Best of those who remember and mention and of those who are remembered and mentioned,

2. O He Who is the Best of those who give thanks and of those who are thanked,

3. O He Who is the Best of those who give praise and of those who are praised,

4. O He Who is the Best of those who witness and of those who are witnessed,

5. O He Who is the Best of those who call, and of those who are called,

6. O He Who is the Best of those who answer calls and of those whose call is accepted,

7. O He Who is the Best of those who familiarize and of those who are familiarized,

8. O He Who is the Best of friends and companions,

يَا خَيْرَ مَقْصُودٍ وَمَطْلُوبٍ ۞

يَا خَيْرَ حَبِيبٍ وَمَحْبُوبٍ ۞

سُبْحَانَكَ يَا لَا إِلٰهَ إِلَّا أَنْتَ الْأَمَانَ الْأَمَانَ
خَلِّصْنَا مِنَ النَّارِ ۞٩٤

يَا مَنْ هُوَ لِمَنْ دَعَاهُ مُجِيبٌ ۞

يَا مَنْ هُوَ لِمَنْ أَطَاعَهُ حَبِيبٌ ۞

يَا مَنْ هُوَ لِمَنْ أَحَبَّهُ قَرِيبٌ ۞

يَا مَنْ هُوَ بِمَنْ أَرَادَهُ عَلِيمٌ ۞

يَا مَنْ هُوَ لِمَنْ رَجَاهُ كَرِيمٌ ۞

يَا مَنْ هُوَ بِمَنْ عَصَاهُ حَلِيمٌ ۞

يَا مَنْ هُوَ فِي حِلْمِهِ حَكِيمٌ ۞

9. O He Who is the Best of those who are longed for and sought after,

10. O He Who is the Best of those who love and of those who are loved,

All-Glorified are You; there is no deity but You!
Mercy! Mercy! Save us from the Fire!

95

1. O He Who answers those who pray to Him,

2. O He Who loves and is loved by those who obey Him,

3. O He Who is close to those who love Him,

4. O He Who knows well those who desire Him,

5. O He Who is munificent to those who are hopeful of Him,

6. O He Who shows forbearance and lenience toward those who rebel against Him without hastening to punish them,

7. O He Who is wise in His forbearance and lenience,

يَا مَنْ هُوَ فِي حُكْمِهِ عَظِيمٌ ۞

يَا مَنْ هُوَ فِي عَظَمَتِهِ رَحِيمٌ ۞

يَا مَنْ هُوَ فِي إِحْسَانِهِ قَدِيمٌ ۞

سُبْحَانَكَ يَا لَا إِلٰهَ إِلَّا أَنْتَ الْأَمَانَ الْأَمَانَ

خَلِّصْنَا مِنَ النَّارِ ۹٥

وَأَسْأَلُكَ بِأَسْمَائِكَ يَا مُسَبِّبُ ۞ يَا مُقَرِّبُ ۞

يَا مُعَقِّبُ ۞ يَا مُقَلِّبُ ۞ يَا مُقَدِّرُ ۞ يَا مُرَتِّبُ ۞

يَا مُرَغِّبُ ۞ يَا مُذَكِّرُ ۞ يَا مُكَوِّنُ ۞ يَا مُتَكَبِّرُ ۞

سُبْحَانَكَ يَا لَا إِلٰهَ إِلَّا أَنْتَ الْأَمَانَ الْأَمَانَ

خَلِّصْنَا مِنَ النَّارِ ۹٦

يَا مَنْ لَا يَشْغَلُهُ سَمْعٌ عَنْ سَمْعٍ ۞

٨٤

8. O He Who is supreme and mighty in His rule and judgment,
9. O He Who is merciful in His might,
10. O He Who is eternal in His favoring,

All-Glorified are You; there is no deity but You!
Mercy! Mercy! Save us from the Fire!

96

I entreat You by Your Names:
1. O the Causer of causes, (Who creates the causes of everything,)
2. O He Who draws closer to Himself whomever He wills,
3. O the All-Pursuing Who makes things follow one another in His wisdom and brings every affair to an end,
4. O the All-Altering and Turning Who changes things into other things and transforms things from one state to another,
5. O the All-Determining (Who determines a particular being, life, nature, and goal for every creature,)
6. O the All-Arranging,
7. O Giver of desire (Who draws everything to Himself and to what is good for it,)
8. O the All-Reminding (Who instructs His servants to keep away from evil and to turn toward good,)
9. O Giver of existence (Who does whatever He wills with the single command of "Be!",
10. O He Who has exclusive right to all greatness,

All-Glorified are You; there is no deity but You!
Mercy! Mercy! Save us from the Fire!

97

1. O He Who is able to hear one voice while simultaneously hearing another,
2. O He Who is able to perform one deed while simultaneously performing another,

يَا مَنْ لَا يَمْنَعُهُ فِعْلٌ عَنْ فِعْلٍ ۞

يَا مَنْ لَا يُلْهِيهِ قَوْلٌ عَنْ قَوْلٍ ۞

يَا مَنْ لَا يَغْلَطُهُ سُؤَالٌ عَنْ سُؤَالٍ ۞

يَا مَنْ لَا يُبْرِمُهُ إِلْحَاحُ الْمُلِحِّينَ ۞

يَا مَنْ شَرَحَ بِالْإِسْلَامِ صُدُورَ الْمُؤْمِنِينَ ۞

يَا مَنْ أَطَابَ بِذِكْرِهِ قُلُوبَ الْمُخْبِتِينَ ۞

يَا مَنْ لَا يَغِيبُ عَنْ قُلُوبِ الْمُشْتَاقِينَ ۞

يَا مَنْ هُوَ غَايَةُ مُرَادِ الْمُرِيدِينَ ۞

يَا مَنْ لَا يَخْفَى عَلَيْهِ شَيْءٌ فِي الْعَالَمِينَ ۞

سُبْحَانَكَ يَا لَا إِلَهَ إِلَّا أَنْتَ الْأَمَانَ الْأَمَانَ
خَلِّصْنَا مِنَ النَّارِ ۞

3. O He Who is able to utter one word while simultaneously uttering another,

4. O He Who is able to answer a call and a request while simultaneously responding to another,

5. O He Who is not tired by the persistence of those who constantly ask,

6. O He Who opens the hearts of believers to Islam and exhilarates them with it,

7. O He Who purifies and makes whole the hearts of His modest servants with remembrance of Him,

8. O He Who is never distant from the hearts of those who long for Him,

9. O He Who is the supreme goal of those who are seeking,

10. O He to Whom nothing in the universe is hidden,

All-Glorified are You; there is no deity but You!
Mercy! Mercy! Save us from the Fire!

يَا مَنْ هُوَ عِلْمُهُ سَابِقٌ ۞

يَا مَنْ هُوَ وَعْدُهُ صَادِقٌ ۞

يَا مَنْ هُوَ لُطْفُهُ ظَاهِرٌ ۞

يَا مَنْ هُوَ أَمْرُهُ غَالِبٌ ۞

يَا مَنْ هُوَ كِتَابُهُ مُحْكَمٌ ۞

يَا مَنْ هُوَ قَضَاؤُهُ كَائِنٌ ۞

يَا مَنْ هُوَ قُرْآنُهُ مَجِيدٌ ۞

يَا مَنْ هُوَ مُلْكُهُ قَدِيمٌ ۞

يَا مَنْ هُوَ فَضْلُهُ مُقِيمٌ ۞

يَا مَنْ هُوَ عَرْشُهُ عَظِيمٌ ۞

سُبْحَانَكَ يَا لَا إِلٰهَ إِلَّا أَنْتَ الْأَمَانَ الْأَمَانَ

98

1. O He Whose knowledge is prior to everything,
2. O He Whose promise is true,
3. O He Whose favors are manifest,
4. O He Whose command is always prevalent,
5. O He Whose Book is firm and sound,
6. O He Whose judgment and decree are executed,
7. O He Whose Qur'an is noble and sublime,
8. O He Whose sovereignty is eternal,
9. O He Whose grace is everlasting,
10. O He Whose Supreme Divine Throne is of ultimate sublimity,

All-Glorified are You; there is no deity but You!
Mercy! Mercy! Save us from the Fire!

خَلِّصْنَا مِنَ النَّارِ ۹۸

يَا رَبَّ الْأَرْبَابِ ۞ يَا مُفَتِّحَ الْأَبْوَابِ ۞

يَا مُسَبِّبَ الْأَسْبَابِ ۞ يَا مُعْطِيَ الثَّوَابِ ۞

يَا مُلْهِمَ الصَّوَابِ ۞ يَا مُنْشِئَ السَّحَابِ ۞

يَا شَدِيدَ الْعِقَابِ ۞ يَا سَرِيعَ الْحِسَابِ ۞

يَا مَنْ لَهُ الْإِيَابُ ۞ يَا غَفُورُ يَا تَوَّابُ ۞

سُبْحَانَكَ يَا لَا إِلَهَ إِلَّا أَنْتَ الْأَمَانَ الْأَمَانَ

خَلِّصْنَا مِنَ النَّارِ ۹۹

وَأَسْأَلُكَ بِأَسْمَائِكَ يَا رَبَّنَا ۞ يَا إِلَهَنَا ۞

يَا سَيِّدَنَا ۞ يَا مَوْلَانَا ۞ يَا نَاصِرَنَا ۞ يَا حَافِظَنَا ۞

يَا قَادِرَنَا ۞ يَا رَازِقَنَا ۞ يَا دَلِيلَنَا ۞ يَا مُغِيثَنَا ۞

٨٧

1. O the Lord of lords,
2. O He Who opens all doors,
3. O the true Causer of causes and their Creator,
4. O He Who gives goodness and rewards,
5. O He Who inspires what is correct and proper,
6. O the Creator and Maker of the clouds,
7. O He Whose punishment is severe,
8. O He Who is the Most Swift in reckoning,
9. O He to Whom return is destined,
10. O the All-Forgiving, O the Acceptor of repentance,

All-Glorified are You; there is no deity but You!
Mercy! Mercy! Save us from the Fire!

100

I entreat You by Your Names:

1. O our Lord,
2. O our Deity,
3. O our Owner,
4. O our Guardian,
5. O our Helper,
6. O our Preserver,
7. O our (Lord) Whose Power dominates everything,
8. O our Provider,
9. O our Guide,
10. O our Succorer and Deliverer,

All-Glorified are You; there is no deity but You!
Mercy! Mercy! Save us from the Fire!

سُبْحَانَكَ يَا اللهُ لَا إِلَهَ إِلَّا أَنْتَ الْأَمَانُ الْأَمَانُ
خَلِّصْنَا مِنَ النَّارِ ۝١٠٠

اَللّٰهُمَّ رَبَّنَا ۝ خَلِّصْنَا ۝ وَأَجِرْنَا ۝
وَنَجِّنَا مِنَ النَّارِ ۝ وَعَافِنَا وَاعْفُ عَنَّا
وَأَدْخِلْنَا الْجَنَّةَ دَارَ قُدْسِكَ مَعَ الْأَبْرَارِ ۝
بِعَفْوِكَ يَا مُجِيرُ ۝ بِفَضْلِكَ يَا غَفَّارُ ۝
وَأَسْأَلُكَ بِحَقِّ هٰذِهِ الْأَسْمَاءِ الْكَرِيمَةِ الشَّرِيفَةِ
وَالصِّفَاتِ الْجَلِيلَةِ اللَّطِيفَةِ أَنْ تُصَلِّيَ
عَلَى سَيِّدِنَا مُحَمَّدٍ وَعَلَى اٰلِهِ وَصَحْبِهِ بِعَدَدِ
حَسَنَاتِ مُحَمَّدٍ بِسْمِ اللهِ ۝ حَسْبِيَ اللهُ
لَا إِلَهَ إِلَّا اللهُ ۝ شَهِدَ اللهُ ۝ قُلْ هُوَ اللهُ ۝

ماشَاءَاللهُ ۞ رَبِّيَ اللهُ ۞ تَبَارَكَ اللهُ ۞

تَعَالَى اللهُ ۞ تَوَكَّلْتُ عَلَى اللهِ

فَسَيَكْفِيكَهُمُ اللهُ وَهُوَ السَّمِيعُ الْعَلِيمُ ۞

سُبْحَانَكَ يَا لَا إِلَهَ إِلَّا أَنْتَ الْأَمَانَ الْأَمَانَ

لَا أُحْصِي ثَنَاءً عَلَيْكَ أَنْتَ كَمَا أَثْنَيْتَ

عَلَى نَفْسِكَ ۞ يَا اللهُ ۞ يَا رَحْمَنُ ۞ يَا رَحِيمُ ۞

يَا غَفُورُ ۞ يَا شَكُورُ ۞ أَسْأَلُكَ بِمَا أَحْصَيْتَهُ

عَلَيْكَ مِنْ أَسْمَائِكَ الْحُسْنَى وَصِفَاتِكَ الْعُلْيَا

وَكَلِمَاتِكَ التَّامَّةِ أَنْ تَغْفِرَ لِي وَلِوَالِدَيَّ

وَلِجَمِيعِ الْمُؤْمِنِينَ وَالْمُؤْمِنَاتِ وَالْمُسْلِمِينَ

وَالْمُسْلِمَاتِ الْأَحْيَاءِ مِنْهُمْ وَالْأَمْوَاتِ

وَتَرْحَمَنَا رَحْمَةً تُغْنِينَا بِهَا عَنْ رَحْمَةِ

مَنْ سِوَاكَ مِنْ خَلْقِكَ وَأَنْ تَقْضِىَ حَوَائِجَنَا

وَتُعْطِينَا سُؤَالَنَا فِى الدُّنْيَا وَالْآخِرَةِ

وَتَخْتِمَ لَنَا بِالسَّعَادَةِ وَالشَّهَادَةِ وَالْكَرَامَةِ

وَالْبُشْرَى عِنْدَ فِرَاقِ الدُّنْيَا وَتَجْزِىَ

مُحَمَّدًا صَلَّى اللهُ عَلَيْهِ وَسَلَّمَ عَنَّا مَا هُوَ أَهْلُهُ

وَمُسْتَحَقُّهُ ۞ وَأَنْ لَا تَكِلَنَا إِلَى أَنْفُسِنَا

طَرْفَةَ عَيْنٍ وَلَا إِلَى أَحَدٍ مِنْ خَلْقِكَ ۞ وَتُصْلِحَ

لَنَا شَأْنَنَا وَأَنْ تَحْرُسَنَا بِعَيْنِكَ الَّتِى لَا تَنَامُ

وَتَحْفَظَنَا بِرُكْنِكَ الَّذِى لَا يُرَامُ يَا ذَا الْجَلَالِ

وَالْإِكْرَامِ وَأَنْ تَصْرِفَ عَنَّا وَعَمَّنْ عُلِّقَ
عَلَيْهِ هَذِهِ الْأَسْمَاءُ آفَةَ الْجِنِّ وَالْإِنْسِ
وَالشَّيَاطِينِ ۞ وَزَلْزَلَةَ الْأَرْضِ وَدَكَّةَ
الْجِبَالِ مِنْ خَشْيَتِهِ ۞ وَآفَةَ الطَّاعُونِ
وَالْوَبَاءِ وَعَيْنَ السُّوءِ وَوَجَعَ الْجَوَارِحِ
وَسَائِرَ الْآفَاتِ ۞ وَتَحْفَظَنَا مِنْ كُلِّ شَرٍّ
وَسُوءٍ ۞ وَتَرْزُقَنَا السَّلَامَةَ وَالْعَافِيَةَ
وَالْخَيْرَ فِي الدُّنْيَا وَالْآخِرَةِ بِرَحْمَتِكَ
يَا أَرْحَمَ الرَّاحِمِينَ وَصَلَّى اللهُ عَلَى سَيِّدِنَا
مُحَمَّدٍ وَآلِهِ وَصَحْبِهِ أَجْمَعِينَ ۞

 وَالْحَمْدُ لِلَّهِ رَبِّ الْعَالَمِينَ

Concluding Prayer

O God, O our Lord, save us, protect us, and deliver us from the Fire! Bestow on us well-being, forgive us, and place us in Paradise, Your pure and clean abode, along with the godly, through Your forgiveness, O, the All-Protecting, and through Your grace O the All-Forgiving!

I ask You, for the sake of these noble and honorable Names and these exalted and gracious Attributes of Yours, to bestow blessings on Prophet Muhammad, his Family and Companions, to the number of the good works of Muhammad!

In the name of God. God is sufficient for me. There is no deity but God. God bears witness to everything.

Say: He – (He is) God. What wonders God wills and whatever He wills comes to be. My Lord is God. God is Blessed and Supreme. God is All-Exalted. I put my trust in God and I rely on Him. God suffices against them. He is the All-Hearing and the All-Knowing.

All-Glorified are You, O, God, Who is the sole Deity! Mercy! Mercy! I am unable to praise You as You praise Yourself. O God, O the All-Merciful, O the All-Compassionate, O the All-Forgiving, O the All-Responsive to the gratitude of His servants.

I ask You, for the sake of Your All-Beautiful Names, Your All-Exalted Attributes, and complete Words, by which You mention and with which describe Yourself, to forgive me, my parents, all believers, and all Muslims, be they dead or alive,

male or female, and to bestow on us such mercy that we will never need the mercy of anyone else from among Your creation. I also ask You to meet all our needs and grant our requests in both this world and the Hereafter, and to grant us a beautiful end with bliss, martyrdom, nobility, liberality and eternal glad tidings when we depart from this world.

Also, give due rewards to Prophet Muhammad, upon him be peace and blessings, to the extent that He deserves, in return for the good deeds he did for us.

Please do not leave us even for a second with our carnal souls, nor with any of your creatures. Make sound and whole all of our states and affairs, and guide, protect, and look after us with Your never-sleeping eye, preserving us with Your support, never abandoning us, O the One of Majesty and Grace!

Avert from us any disaster that may be caused by the jinn, humans, or devils, or by earthquakes, the shattering of mountains out of their fear of God, and plagues, pestilences, the evil eye, and all other diseases, pains, or disasters. Preserve us from every evil and vice!

And, for the sake of Your Mercy, O the Most Compassionate of the compassionate, provide us with salvation, well-being, and goodness in this world as well as in the Hereafter.

Bestow Your peace and blessings on our master Muhammad, and on his Family and Companions altogether! All praise be to God, the Lord of the worlds!

التجويد الميسر